David D. Dennis

FATAL ACCOUNTS

The Audacity of an Adventist
Auditor's Quest for Transparency

Published by

Adventist Today

Library of Congress Cataloging-in-Publication Data

Fatal Accounts: The Audacity of an Adventist Auditor's Quest for Transparency
David D. Dennis

p. cm.
Includes index
ISBN 0-9786141-7-8 (paperback)
1. Seventh-day Adventists—Clergy.
2. Seventh-day Adventists—History.

ISBN 0-9786141-7-8 (paperback)

© 2009 David D. Dennis

davedennis@verizon.net

Printed in the United States of America
Adventist Today
Riverside, California

"The corruptions of the world always make their way into religious establishments, and once they do, religious authorities lose their credibility. 'Shortcomings' and hypocrisies that would be bad enough in secular politicians are even worse in clerics."

Jon Maecham, *Newsweek*, June 29, 2009

Table of Contents

Dedication

This book is dedicated to Charlotte, my faithful companion of nearly a half-century, along with our two great children, Cheryl and Sam, all of whom loyally stood by me with love and encouragement when the going was tough and others mocked and jeered.

Foreword

For more than 20 years I have known Dave Dennis. He had been directing the General Conference of Seventh-day Adventists Auditing Service for some 10 years when, in 1986, I came to the General Conference Biblical Research Institute. Throughout our years together, I found Dave to be a genuine Christian gentleman, deeply interested in the spiritual and financial welfare of his denomination, as well as the local congregations where he worshiped.

Auditing is a bit like piloting airplanes. It involves hours of boredom, interspersed with moments of sheer terror. It's tedious, but every now and then the auditor finds out-of-policy entries and investments, and this can lead to confrontations.

To the best of my knowledge Dave has always been an outstanding auditor, and because on occasion he found and reported irregular financial conduct on the part of some Church leaders, they became unenthusiastic about his work.

An attempt was made to remove him from office during the General Conference session in Indianapolis, Indiana, in 1990, but objections arose, and a group of Dave's fellow auditors appeared before the committee, supporting the integrity of Dave's work. Dave was restored to his position, largely because his professional colleagues valued his work and qualifications.

During that time, two local conference presidents told me that they did not approve of Dave's auditing methods. But neither questioned his honesty or his commitment to the Church.

Dave's woes had only begun, however. A General Conference official, while on vacation in 1994, heard it rumored that a woman was claiming that she and Dave had engaged in an improper sexual relationship. Both Dave and his wife knew the emotionally fragile accuser well, and in fact had agreed to allow her to stay in their Singapore home, during a period of time when it was feared that she might otherwise become suicidal.

But by 1994, the woman had been divorced once, and her second marriage was in trouble. So she had sought the help of a counselor, where she "recovered her memory" of an affair with Dave—an affair in an unnamed hotel, some 12 years earlier, when Dave was traveling in the company of his wife. The accusation was, at worst, a lie; at best, it was the product of an overactive imagination.

Ordinarily the denomination gives its valued employees ample opportunity to respond to accusations, especially in cases, such as Dave's, where the accuser has personal reasons for bringing the accusation but has absolutely no physical evidence, and where details are unconvincingly sketchy.

But powerful forces in the General Conference wanted Dave removed from office, and the determination was made that the woman's testimony would be used to try to persuade him to quit. This backfired, however, when Dave resolutely refused to resign, because both he and Charlotte knew the accusation to be false.

So Dave's accusers took the next step and convened a small committee of a half-dozen people, consisting of the woman and her supporter, Dave and his supporter, and a couple of officiating General Conference officers.

Then a special meeting of the General Conference Committee was called to decide the issue, and though transcripts from the smaller committee were promised to the committee members, these never appeared. Instead, the committee was informed that Dave had not conclusively proved that the affair had not taken place, and that therefore he should be terminated.

Dave was grudgingly allowed to read a five-minute defense, then was sent from the room, while the committee discussed the situation for a total of seven hours. To terminate Dave would require a two-thirds plurality, and finally, perhaps from sheer physical fatigue, the motion to terminate him squeaked by with a less-than-70 percent "yes" count.

Dave was summarily rebuffed when he officially requested the right to appeal his case to a grievance committee, so at last he brought legal action against the General Conference for defamation and wrongful termination. The conduct of the legal phase of this process was even more irregular than what had occurred before. A very expensive legal team from three D.C. law firms spent scores of billable hours in a grueling week, taking testimony in depositions by Dave and his family members. But when the time came for the General Conference officials most directly involved in the matter to be deposed, they hid behind the First Amendment privilege and refused to testify under oath.

The officials and attorneys representing the General Conference claimed to have a strong case against Dave, but spent seven years battling at great expense to keep the case from being tried. Using (in my opinion, abusing) the First Amendment separation of Church and state, Church officials claimed they were immune from prosecution. Even after failing in the Maryland State Supreme Court, the General Conference kept spending money and appealing until the case was remanded to a lower court judge, who agreed that Church officials could not be tried for malpractice they may have committed in the line of duty. (One wonders if the judge would make such a ruling today, in the wake of Catholic clergy now routinely being tried in civil court for sexual abuse of parishioners.)

But Dave did receive a measure of vindication, when the General Conference official most responsible for his dismissal was himself forced to resign—on grounds that he had conducted irregular financial affairs outside of Church channels. It now became quite evident why he had wanted Dave out of the way.

I have chronicled these events as I observed them. Interpretations may differ, but I believe this general outline of the historical process is reasonably accurate. Dave was guilty of no crime other than trying to preserve the fiscal integrity of the Church's accounts. As a faithful servant of the Church, he served it well for nearly 35 years. A great injustice was done him, and he deserves an apology from current Church leadership. Whether an apology comes or not, Dave soldiers on as a faithful servant, active in his local Adventist congregation and in lockstep with his Master, the Lord Jesus Christ.

William H. Shea, M.D., Ph.D.
Associate Director (retired), Biblical Research Institute
General Conference of SDA
Bristow, Virginia

Preface

Great men spend years penning their memoirs, focusing on their good deeds and notable moments. They know full well that in the annals of eternity, fame is but a vision of the night—a vapor misting over the tapestry of time and space.

I have chosen to write this autobiography, not to claim great accomplishments, but to tell the simple truth about events that drove me from a lifetime of service to my Church—a Church I have supported and loved all my life.

I draw my inspiration from a lowly carpenter's Son who was despised and rejected of men, falsely accused, and condemned in a charade of a trial. He was deserted and slandered by his colleagues and friends, and His name was trampled in the mud of Golgotha.

I have experienced only a taste of what He suffered, but His story strengthens me to write—for I, like Him, am a reformer by temperament.

I was born into a Seventh-day Adventist home, the last of three children. At age 13 I joined the Church and have remained a staunch member throughout life—for more than 57 years. My parents sacrificed to send me to Adventist parochial schools for most of my elementary and college studies.

After I graduated with a degree in business administration, the Church recruited me to serve in finance overseas — during the 1960s and early 1970s, we made our home variously in Uruguay, Chile, Indonesia, and Singapore. Though I worked primarily as an accountant, treasurer, and auditor, I also preached evangelistic series in Asia, Canada, the United States, Africa, and Europe. During the final 19 years of my nearly-35-year career, I served as director of internal auditing at the Church's world headquarters, where I uncovered financial corruption related to the Church's president and of one of his vice presidents. I, in turn, was summarily terminated in 1994, which effectively stopped me from presenting an official report at the then-upcoming 1995 Quinquennial Session of the General Conference.

To expedite my firing before the 1995 Session, the president brought forward false charges that I had engaged in sexual misconduct and, in effect, treated me as "guilty until proven innocent." Church administrators worldwide were apprised of my supposed transgressions, and my name and reputation were thoroughly trashed.

In this book I summarize my life, leading up to that time, and show compelling reasons why false allegations were brought against me, and why the firing ultimately was motivated by opposition to the reforms I was advocating.

It is not a pleasant story, though I have made every effort to be accurate and to forgive those who have brought this evil, not only upon me, but upon my wife of nearly 50 years, and upon my children and grandchildren.

Why I Write

Three primary reasons compel me to write. First, because I was an elected Church employee, the legal system in the United States refused to consider my plea for vindication — citing issues of separation of church and state. Second, I hope to remain an articulate influence for reform in the cumbersome system we call Adventist Church governance. And, finally, in exposing the treatment I received, I hope in some way to help protect other reformers rising now and in the future.

I remain an active member of the Seventh-day Adventist Church — my local congregation does not give any credibility whatever to the charges the General Conference brought against me. In turn, during the past 15 years, I have learned to appreciate the contrasting differences between the reprehensible behavior of leadership and the beauty of the Adventist message. Within five years of my firing, my primary antagonist, Robert Folkenberg, was himself driven from office when he admitted to improper financial dealings. But his fall brought me no joy — he too was a victim of a system that has grown too unwieldy to be properly managed. It's time for Adventism to turn from its hierarchical style of administration, modeled on the Roman Catholic, and seriously consider a more simplified method of leadership.

Today I am certainly more cautious and, in many ways, wiser than I was as a Church employee. Sadly, my children suffered intense disillusionment as they witnessed the treatment their mother and I received. As a family, we pray for change in the Adventist Church. Our story is but one among thousands of would-be reformers who challenge the status quo. Our hearts and prayers go out to them all.

Notable

The St. Louis 2005 58th General Conference Session Supplement of the *Adventist Review* published the following statements of four named and voted delegates alerting fellow colleagues to the problems the church has with "Servant Leaders"

"Sometimes the auditors find discrepancies in financial matters. Their reports often have explicit recommendations but the administrators do little or nothing to rectify these errors. I have had individuals say that they are not concerned with the auditors report because they are connected with the powers that be and will remain in office.

"At times integrity, truthfulness, honesty, and sincerity are not evident in an entity; it becomes impossible for an individual to point out the wrongs, because deceit, dishonesty, and lack of sincerity have already become systemic. When a group of individuals create and nurture an atmosphere of corruption, and when institutionalized corruption is accepted as a way of life, what means are left to the individual seeking change?

"People are unwilling to follow incompetent leaders.

"I will get right to the point. Our people have lost confidence in the leadership of the church from top to bottom."

Chapter 1:
The Ax Falls

I can still vividly picture the General Conference (GC) committee room in my mind's eye, that far-off day in October 1994. Former GC vice president, the late Charles Hirsch, coordinated the process of my Church trial. From his introduction before the hearing, I could tell he had already made up his mind how this would end. I was given no advance information about who would be attending the meeting, but Attorney Walter Carson had — as it turned out, falsely — promised me that he would not be directly involved. Even so, this was a mere formality; the case had been decided in advance.

My prosecutor, Vice President Kenneth Mittleider, brought in Barbara Middag, his private secretary of many years, to serve as recording secretary. In typical denominational committee style, a panel of hand-picked judges sat to rule against me, including my old colleague from South America, Rowena Rick; Susan Sickler, a General Conference Committee member from Ohio; Rogelio Weiss, a Hispanic who had worked with Mittleider in the Potomac Conference; and Richard Barron, an African American minister.

On the far end of the meeting room in the GC complex sat Elizabeth "Beth" Heisler Olson Adels and her psychological counselor; a box of Kleenex tissue was strategically placed nearby. I was now told that anyone who would testify on my behalf could not be present at this trial—a problem, since I saw my wife, Charlotte's personal testimony as vital to my defense. So instead of being allowed to sit with me through the proceeding, she had to wait outside until it was time for her to speak.

So at the last moment, I invited my erstwhile friend, the late Kenneth Wood and former *Adventist Review* editor and chairman of the White Estate board, to sit with me. This later backfired, when Wood himself pressured me to resign my position, and turned against me when I refused to do so. I had not realized that he and then-Church President Robert Folkenberg were close friends. In fact, Wood had promoted and helped to fund a wall mural by artist Elfred Lee, in which the figure of Robert Folkenberg leads the Adventist faithful on a narrow pathway to heaven! Derived from a vision recounted by Church founder Ellen White, this painting now hangs in the White Estate offices at the General Conference.

At the back of the room, guiding the proceedings, were my prosecutors, Mittleider and Carson. With the somber pageantry of a funeral, the session opened with a devotional, appropriately based on Matthew 18, but conveniently skipping verse 15, where Christians are commanded to go first directly to their brothers and sisters when aggrieved. Carson then launched into an eloquent, 90-minute attack against me and my family.

He quoted heavily from a notarized document he and Beth had created, in which they recounted her supposed memories of sexual activity with me. Carson also cited letters provided by GC Security Chief, Melvin Seard, who had partnered with the prosecution throughout. Seard himself had carried on an adulterous relationship with the GC switchboard operator, Christine Seek Metcalf Pyle Baerg, a year or more earlier, and mistakenly believed I had exposed that relationship. Interestingly enough, Seard, a light-skinned African American, had been exonerated by the GC Personnel Committee, which was sensitive to any appearance of racially motivated disciplinary action.

Suddenly, now, this man produced fabricated letters that I had supposedly written to his former love interest, Baerg — letters that Mittleider and Carson said proved that I had flirted with Baerg, and was therefore, by inference, a confirmed philanderer. Yet these letters were never submitted to experts to determine their authenticity, and neither Seard nor Baerg testified about the matter under oath.

Next Beth haltingly told her story, generously drawing from the box of Kleenex. She retracted her earlier accusations that I had given her erotic backrubs as a teenage guest in my home, 20 years before. These were of no erotic consequence, she now said (contrary to what she and Carson had written in her affidavit). She also now said that, upon reflection, her allegation that I had groped her in Singapore had been misconstrued in the affidavit. But she stuck to her story that she had met me at a motel near her Tennessee home some 12 years before. So, now, her case hinged entirely on whether she could prove that this rendezvous had occurred — something Charlotte and I knew she could not do, for the encounter had never occurred.

Beth said that psychological therapy had helped her recall this long-forgotten rendezvous — that 12 years before we had met for sexual purposes in a hotel, though the therapy had been unable to help her recall the name of the motel. But she testified that through therapy she could now recall that early in the afternoon, after the tryst, I had pushed her from the motel room and told her she could not spend the night with me.

I was then allowed to question her, from across the room, and I chose to concentrate on the kind of psychiatric therapy that had suddenly brought these memories to light. Among other things, she denied ever being hypnotized.

Beth then brought forward a woman named Maggie as her witness — a woman who said she had babysat Beth's young children while she was with me at the motel. Maggie said that Beth had phoned her that evening from the motel room to inquire if the children were well. While Maggie admitted that at that point she had never met me, she now testified that she had recognized my voice over the phone, in the background as Beth asked about the welfare of the children. Maggie also could not explain how, if Beth had left my room early in the afternoon after I locked her out, my voice could still be heard.

Next Charlotte was invited in from an outer room to speak on my behalf. Confident and unfaltering, she gave her testimony, which Mittleider twice interrupted with the words, "You're lying."

But Charlotte soldiered on, pointing out that she had been physically present with me during times when it was now alleged that I had been involved in sexual misconduct. I could see that Charlotte's confident testimony angered Mittleider, and that he was now becoming extremely concerned that the flimsy assumptions on which he had tried to build his case were crumbling. Charlotte resolutely pointed out that Beth, while a troubled ward in our home, would seek guidance from her into the wee hours of many mornings. She made it clear that Beth had shared a bedroom with our daughter, and that no one in our household had ever heard, seen, or been told of anything suspicious involving the 15-year-old and me. Then Charlotte turned and spoke directly to Beth and asked her why, if her charges of my misconduct were true, she had not brought them up earlier to her two spouses? Why all of a sudden? Why only now? Beth had no response.

Thus the hearing ended, and Mittleider and Carson met with the hand-picked judges and together they recommended to the General Conference Committee that, under the circumstances, I should be terminated. Beth's story, they wrote, seemed believable, but was inconclusive. But not to be denied, Mittleider later edited the document to state explicitly that I had been found guilty as charged! This altered copy was presented during my court depositions, and I still have a copy.

The altered report was presented, in my absence, to the GC Administrative Committee, a meeting to which I was invited at the last minute—but I declined to attend and chose to wait and make my case at the upcoming GC Committee meeting, December 22, 1994. When I showed up at that meeting with my 31-year-old son, many of my colleagues seemed surprised.

There I was grudgingly allowed to read a statement, which I requested be affixed to the GC actions of the day. That request was denied, and I was ordered to leave the meeting room while the committee discussed whether or not I should be fired.

Then for seven hours Mittleider, Carson, and Folkenberg belabored my case, trying to drum up the necessary two-thirds majority to oust me. They finally succeeded, though the vote was less than 70 percent in favor of my termination. But it was a two-thirds vote—the brethren had prevailed!

I was interested in the recorded comment of one committee member, who urged his fellows to vote me out because I was so "disliked." And later in court proceedings, former-GC president Neal Wilson would tell the judge that I was fired for "lack of people skills." This confirmed in my mind that my firing was essentially political—that my outspokenness and incorruptibility in financial and procedural matters was really at the heart of the case.

Beth's testimony, however flimsy and implausible, had weakened my position just enough to permit my ouster. It was all a set-up, and I knew it.

On December 24 I was told of the vote to terminate me, "effective immediately," but that due to the prevailing holiday spirit, my salary would be paid through December 31, when my medical benefits would also cease. So, since the Church is not required to contribute to the state's unemployment fund, at age 56 I was left with no job, the smear of "sexual misconduct" associated with my name, no employment opportunities, and no health benefits.

But I felt certain that in the heart of Jesus, who too had been falsely accused, there was no rejoicing. He too had been tried before the Sanhedrin's council and been mocked by the very ones He had tried all His life to help.

I reflected on my humble beginnings in the Depression-era Midwest, on my college life with a double-major in religion and business — then on to pastoring, conference treasury work, and nearly two decades of missionary service. For years, powerful enemies had been seeking ways to remove me from my position as chief auditor of the worldwide Seventh-day Adventist Church. At last, after many failures, those enemies had succeeded. But paradoxically, I now felt very close to my Savior. I was bloodied, but unbowed.

Chapter 2:
From Robinson Hill to Peanut Hill

Life began for me four miles west of Macon, Missouri, along a bumpy gravel track, on 60 acres of property known as Robinson Hill — at least that's what my parents called the area when I was born there in the summer of 1938. Not too much has changed since. Charlotte and I drove there recently and found that the old wood house has been rebuilt and expanded into a luxury home of a prosperous local attorney. His Dobermans eyed us suspiciously, as we examined the site of our family's old storage cellar and well. But aside from the new house, the property appears unchanged in the 70 years since I was born there. Lush growths of timber cover the rolling terrain, bisected by a little stream. Even now I can picture my dad with his team of horses, turning the soil.

Memories fade, but my early life remains vivid. I was the youngest — a distinct afterthought — of three children born to Sam and Nadine Dennis, and my sister, Geraldine, was already engaged to marry when I was born. She and her new husband, Archie March, later that year moved to Rockford, Illinois. When I was three, my brother, Paul, was drafted and shipped to Europe to fight the Nazis.

My parents noticed that I suffered from hay fever, which would begin in late summer, when the pollens were at their peak, and progress to asthma as the days grew colder. Medical science in those days had no effective treatment for asthma, and the doctors told us that I would do better if we moved to a higher, dryer climate. So my desperate parents sold the farm and took me by train to live in Colorado.

Dad soon found work in a large warehouse in Pueblo; but within a few months mother's health began to decline, due to the high altitude, which exacerbated her high blood pressure. We moved to Kansas.
The train took us through the cowboy town of Dodge City, where Dad got off to look for work, while Mom and I rode on with Grandma (mother's mother had come to live with us) to stay with family in Missouri, until Dad could find work and a house. He attended the Seventh-day Adventist Church in Dodge City, his first Sabbath in town.

My parents had joined the Adventist Church together a few years before, though my father had been baptized as a child, when his parents studied the Bible evenings with neighbors as they milked their cows and did the chores. But after Dad's mother died, he left home and in his struggles in life wandered from the Church. When he met my mother, she was a devout Presbyterian, but later joined him in accepting the "Three Angels' Messages."

Dad asked the Dodge City pastor if there was a church school for me to attend in the area, and was assured that such a school was opening in Garden City, about 50 miles away. Dad boarded a train to Garden City and introduced himself to the local church elder, Alfred Winters, informing him that he intended to settle in town. Alfred, in turn, cautioned him that nobody in town was hiring.

Even so, the next morning Dad got up, dressed, had breakfast, and announced that he was off to find work. "Jobs are scarce," they repeated, but assured him that he was welcome to use their guest room as long as he needed it.

Later that morning, Alfred stopped by the bank and noticed a small crew digging a sewer ditch—and there Dad was, pick and shovel in hand. In the next few months, Dad found various maintenance jobs and rented a small apartment in a rooming house, before sending for my mother and me.

Because the church school had not yet opened, my parents enrolled me as a first-grader in public school, and Mother worked, making alterations at a dry cleaners, during school hours. Dad, meanwhile, found better work as a maintenance man in government projects, and began a trash-hauling service. In a move that predates our ecological sensitivities today, he invited his clients to separate their scraps and leftovers from lighter, dry trash. A local rancher gladly used the scraps and leftovers for hog feed.

Meanwhile, my parents worked with local members to convert an old army barracks into a schoolhouse, and about a year after we arrived in town, I became one of its eight charter students. Shortly after I finished eighth grade, however, the housing project where Dad worked closed, and we transferred to a similar project near Hutchinson, in east-central Kansas, where Dad continued working as a civil servant.

Hutchinson, known for its underground salt mines, was only a short hour's drive from Wichita. I graduated from Hutchinson High and continued my studies at the local junior college, just two blocks from home.

But my parents wanted me to graduate from an Adventist college and were prepared to sacrifice to make it possible. Dad believed that God directly appointed every Church worker— especially ministers—and that it was his and Mom's spiritual duty to urge me back into an Adventist school, where I could prepare to serve the Lord.

My parents had debated whether or not to enroll me in an Adventist boarding academy, but had felt that the influences of a Christian home were more important than those of a boarding school. In retrospect, I'm convinced they made the right choice. Many of my peers who attended boarding schools lost their faith in God. But in public school, I realized I had to stand alone. I would not participate in the school's competitive sports, and attended very few social functions. Dad taught me to play baseball and would attend sporting events with me, and both he and Mom were always available for counsel and companionship. By the time I left home for college, I was prepared to face the temptations of dormitory life.

I enrolled at Union College, in an eastern suburb of Lincoln, Nebraska, known as College View. A five-hour drive from home, it was the nearest Adventist college campus and had been dubbed "Peanut Hill" by neighbors who found profound amusement in our strange eating habits.

In high school I had completed a vocational course in printing and had worked some at a commercial press in the old letterpress system. So

I found work running the college's Heidelberg, a windmill-type press—a job that offered flexible hours and time for me to study while the press ran. There I decided to make printing my life's career and to pursue a degree in business administration, so I could both manage and track the finances of a printing business.

But as my college credits accumulated, helpful friends and faculty encouraged me to switch my major to theology and enter Church ministry, so I scheduled an appointment with a religion department professor. When I explained to him that I felt called to pastoral ministry, he asked me what I was prepared to do in case I was not employed as a pastor. I replied that I was prepared to work in graphic arts or in some area of business. To my surprise, he abruptly ended our interview, asserting that if I could envision doing anything other than ministry, I clearly was not called to be a minister. End of discussion.

Dad passed away from heart disease during my second year in college, and Mom moved to Lincoln to share costs with me in an apartment. Two years later, in 1960, I graduated with honors and was named in *Who's Who in American Colleges and Universities*, with a Bachelor of Science degree in business administration, a degree in religion, and a minor in speech. Thanks to my work at the college press and a successful summer canvassing as a student literature evangelist, I graduated free of debt, with more than enough money left over to buy a new Ford for $2,300. How proud I was of that full-size, four-door sedan! With the rest of the money, Mom and I drove to the West Coast for a short vacation.

A few months before, I had met Charlotte Morris, an attractive student musician, at choir practice before the Christmas holidays. She loved to sing and play solo piano, organ, and marimba, and was a trombonist in the college band. Our eyes met that evening, and electricity traveled between us. We started finding excuses to meet, date, and just spend time together. But too quickly the school year ended and I graduated.

Job offers came—attractive accounting positions—but my parents had always urged me to work for the denomination, and that was my goal.

As I traveled with my mother toward the West Coast in my brand-new Ford, I reflected on the three employment offers I had received. Pacific Press, then in Mountain View, California, had offered me a job in a Church-operated book center; a midwestern Adventist hospital wanted me to fill an administrative position; and the Iowa Conference had offered me a position in treasury that would involve me directly in Church ministry. I accepted that third offer, to work with J. O. McLeod, conference treasurer.

When M. D. Howard, my conference president, learned that I was willing and able to conduct Sabbath speaking appointments, he issued me a ministerial license—which at that time made it extremely unlikely that I would be drafted into the military.

On weekdays I served in the conference office as assistant treasurer/auditor, but on weekends I was told to fill in for a pastor who was away at Seminary. So every-other Sabbath I would speak at a little church in Winterset, for the early morning service, then drive to Guthrie Center for the 11 o'clock service.

On alternate Sabbaths, I would go to Greenfield to preach in the morning and to Creston in the afternoon. How I enjoyed the fellowship!

I remember, in particular, my first Sabbath visit to the Creston church. When I arrived, the members apologized that they had no preacher that day (I seemed so young, they assumed I was a student visiting from Oak Park Academy). Finally, we all shared a laugh when I told them that I had been sent by the conference to be their preacher!

Funds were tight, and my beginning salary was meager—$44 a week, and I had little social life with those my own age.

But I enjoyed other pleasant associations, and I remember J. O. McLeod and his wife, Mattie Mae, as charming, gracious, and hospitable when they'd invite me over for grits on Sunday morning. I'd grown up on Southern fare and loved it!

Meanwhile, my friendship with Charlotte deepened. Absence was making our hearts grow fonder. She was in Colorado for the summer, and since she had completed only one year of college, she planned to return to her studies in the fall. But three more years seemed like an awfully long time, and finally I decided to ask her if she really wouldn't rather begin a life with me. She agreed that life would be better if we were together, and on September 4, 1960, we were married in her home church in Boulder, Colorado. It was a simple, but colorful, service conducted by an old, family pastor and personal friend, L. L. McKinley, who was then Montana Conference president. After a short honeymoon in a borrowed cabin in the Rockies, we moved to Des Moines.

Time passed quickly, and little Cheryl came to bless our home. Then, late in 1961, we received a letter that invited us to serve as foreign missionaries in Uruguay, where I would be cashier-accountant for the South American Division in Montevideo. Since we had never really considered overseas work, my first thought was to decline with a "thank you for thinking of us" letter.

But Larry Smart, my colleague in education and youth work in our office, wisely pointed out that perhaps this was God's will for our lives. How could we ask others to follow Jesus, if we were not willing to go where He led?

After prayerful consideration, we accepted the call, packed our few belongings, and set sail in the winter of 1961 on a freighter from New York City. We sailed across the equator to a suddenly-summer rendez-vous with a small band of our new fellow workers in Montevideo, on New Year's Day.

They stood on the dock to greet us as our vessel moored, and how good it was after more than two weeks in near solitude to see the welcome in the smiles of so many who had come out on a holiday to say "Welcome!"

Chapter 3:
I'll Go Where You Want Me to Go

Montevideo is a clean, quaint, Spanish-speaking city on the Atlantic with a population of primarily Southern European descent, where we settled in and prepared for the many adjustments ahead. We were young—Charlotte had just celebrated her 20th birthday, and I was only 23. We had been told that our youth would help us adjust and master the new language, and this proved to be true. Strange excitement surged through us, as we faced uncertain challenges 5,000 miles from our families back home.

We threw ourselves into our new life, Charlotte valiantly shouldering housework far heavier than she had known back home. Our house on the mission compound was large, with high-maintenance, polished hardwood floors. Little Cheryl needed attention and training, too, and shopping took hours. Uruguay's stores back then offered almost no prepared foods, and fresh produce was available only on Sunday mornings at the *feria* (farmers' market). Survival demanded that we put our rapidly learned new Spanish vocabulary to immediate use. We were now dealing in *pesos,* and Charlotte had to mentally translate their value. Life was not easy!

I too confronted new experiences each day, as *contador* (accountant) for the South American division office. My new boss, Bob Osborn, offered inspiration and challenges. As a rule I rise early, but I found it difficult to get to the office before he did, at 4:30 a.m. His secretary, Carolyn Sibley, mirrored his efficiency and hard work, and could type 100 detailed, dictated letters a day on her old-style, manual typewriter. But still she could not keep up with Osborn, so Osborn would personally type many of his own letters. My predecessor, Karl Bahr, was leaving soon to serve as Bolivia Mission treasurer, and the competent Rowena Rick who had been serving for six years as bookkeeper frankly intimidated me, given her maturity and experience. Deep down, I felt she — not I — deserved to be the *contador.* We were expected to record accounting entries in at least two currencies — the original foreign currency, as well as the local *peso.* What an adjustment!

Meanwhile, we spent at least an hour a day in language study, then put our growing vocabulary to use in the marketplace and church. Neither of us had studied Spanish before, and when invited to sing, we tried hard to pronounce the words properly — though we had no idea what they meant.

What a joy for me, after about 18 months of study, to be able to deliver a worship sermon at the little Curva de Maroñas church. I had virtually committed the whole message to memory, and was amused when a member of the audience assured me afterward that I preached a lot better than I talked!

Early in my career, I had learned that in Church politics those in power protected their jobs by cultivating circles of allies. When we arrived in South America, an old circle was just breaking up, and we found it easy to befriend the newer appointees.

Then our own little Uruguayo arrived, little Samuel (named for my father), in 1963. He weighed nearly 10 pounds, strikingly more than most Uruguayan newborns, and the nurses nicknamed him El Campeón (The Champion). Though he was bald as a bean, to us he was beautiful. We had no personal car, so I would take two-year-old Cheryl on my shoulders and walk the two-and-a-half-mile trek to the British Hospital to visit *Samuelito* and *Mamá*. Our family was now complete.

An invitation to serve as secretary-treasurer of the South Chile Conference in Temuco interrupted our ease in beautiful Montevideo. Again we traveled by ship, this time around Cape Horn, to our new home about 600 miles south of the capital city, Santiago. There we rented one side of a duplex housing unit, with a quiet lawn and large fruit trees.

We found the conference in severe financial straits, but undaunted, we believed that God would give us the vision and strength to succeed, and in less than two years, the budget was balanced and all debts paid.

One wintry Sabbath morning we left a fire going in our sturdy wood-burning stove, while we all attended church, only to receive the urgent message, between services, that our home was on fire. We rushed home to find that we had lost everything. Firemen were doing what they could, but our valuables were all gone — except for our lives, the clothes we wore, and the car we now owned. That evening after Sabbath, we all bought toothbrushes, and the next day visited the local Adventist Development and Relief warehouse to find everyday clothing. A kind woman who owned property out in the country rented us her fully furnished city home, near our office.

We had been in South America for five years, and it was now time to reacquaint ourselves with the homeland and for me to further my education in accounting. For more than a decade the denomination had been urging gospel ministers to take graduate study at the Seminary, but those in its business offices often lacked baccalaureate degrees. This bothered me I wanted to move forward in my accounting skills and had been approved to study for my Master's of Business Administration at the University of Kansas, in Lawrence.

We traveled to the States with a friend from Chile, Alejo Pizarro, to serve as delegates to the 1966 Session of the General Conference, held at Cobo Hall in Detroit. Leaving our children with family in Missouri, we reveled in fellowship with missionary friends and representatives of the world Church, telling them that, yes, we would be returning to Chile in a year, for another term!

But I knew that I faced a possible hitch in those plans. Our furlough would end the following March, but my graduation from the MBA program would not take place until June 1967. Denominational working policy provided for an extension of furlough, for "study purposes." But it used the word "may" rather than "will," and we had learned that in matters of Church politics, nothing should be taken for granted.

In July I settled in to study, and routinely contacted my employers, the General Conference, for permission to extend my study for three extra months. The Secretary in charge of such requests, David Baasch, was himself a veteran missionary to Latin America, and he assured me that such requests were routinely approved.

So what was my surprise when he phoned to tell me that my request had been denied — though he still held out hope that he could persuade the South American Division of my serious commitment to complete the degree.

A few weeks later, just before the 1966 holiday season, Baasch wrote me that South America would definitely not grant the additional three months and that we should prepare to fold our tent and "follow God's leading." He reminded me that God leads through committees, and that the committee had spoken.

This apparent rigidity shocked me, and we prayed about the matter before writing back that, while we concurred that God leads through committees, we believed God also leads us as individuals, and that God's will for my life included completion of this graduate degree, now within our grasp.

This was clearly a "control" situation. I had learned that Church officials who for whatever reason are insecure, often impose inordinate control on others' lives. It seemed I had been branded a rebel, and shortly another letter came from Baasch, advising me without fanfare that I was being relieved of my appointment to the South American Division.

Surprisingly, the very next day a letter came from Duane Johnson, another General Conference Secretary, who had served for many years as a missionary in Southern Asia. Johnson advised me that I had been placed under appointment to the Far Eastern Division, to serve as treasurer of the West Indonesia Union—subject to completion of my degree! The God who had called us as missionaries was still leading in our lives.

I began second semester at the university at the top of my class, and I was actually starting to have fun, spending more time with the kids in the snow—something they had never seen before. Everything seemed to be sailing right along toward graduation. My thesis was ready and already approved by the faculty, on "Inflationary Accounting in South America." As graduation day neared, I prepared to march with some 3,000 other post-baccalaureate students to receive my diploma.

Chapter 4:

Pitching Our Tent Again

By late July we were off again, on Pan American Airways — traveling not south, but west. Our journey included short stops in Hawaii, Japan, Korea, the Philippines, Bangkok, and Singapore — where we visited our new division headquarters. At last we arrived in Jakarta, late one evening, and noted the dark sprawl of the city, with its red-tiled roofs.

The cultural adjustment would be greater for us here than in South America, and we were expected to learn a second new language, Bahasa Indonesia. Charlotte had to adjust to new cooking and entertainment routines, including live-in hospitality for frequent Western visitors, as they passed through.

Since our home on the missionary compound in Jakarta's suburbs was far from the airport, on days when guests came in late at night, I would stay at the office and work until it came time to pick them up. Days were long and the territory vast, with eight local missions, a large hospital with its inherent headaches, a large publishing house, a senior college, and related schools and book centers.

The union was in financial crisis, and inflation was rampant—much worse than what we had known in South America. Prior Church administrators in Indonesia had come to believe that going into debt, under these circumstances, had seemed to make sense, since inflation had the effect of rapidly diminishing the actual indebtedness.

A longtime Southern Baptist missionary to Indonesia told me one day, "It's a full time job just living here, without getting any work done." There was some truth in what he said. Everything seemed more complicated here. There were no prepared foods to buy, and labor-saving household appliances were few. Our children were growing and housekeeping demanded all of Charlotte's time. Almost daily she entertained guests and had to look after the compound's guest rooms. To help her, we finally hired a maid, Mumun (moo-MOON), who helped cook, clean, shop, and look after the children. A devout young Muslim, she served us loyally and well.

We helped establish a little school on the compound, where both our children received good Christian training, as they excelled in their studies.

The exotic fruit, including the king of fruits, the spiny-smelly durian was a daily treat. Besides a half-dozen varieties of mangos, we had jack fruit, rambutans, salak, mangosteen, ducos, and blingbings. We ate rice at least twice daily, with variations of soy bean-based tofu and tempe, and remained healthy.

When our bookkeeper for missionary accounts moved away, Charlotte was conscripted into extra service. Cheryl and Sam were by now in school, and Mumun cared for them after classes. My work required me to travel often, but lengthy absences were few. I also sat on the boards of the hospital, the publishing house, and the senior college, and I was responsible for giving financial counsel to the local missions. So I traveled over our vast archipelago from North Sumatra to Irian Jaya (the west side of New Guinea Island), primarily by air.

Adding to these pressures was lack of time for language study. The Indonesian language is a composite of several tongues, based on Sanskrit, with vocabulary added by former Dutch colonists, and English, Arabic, and Portuguese influences. We found that the Indonesian people learned languages quickly, and many could speak English with us—which, in turn, delayed our mastery of their language.

But through trial and error and a smattering of formal instruction, we learned a fair bit of the language. Indonesian is fun to speak, and we still enjoy it with old friends.

It took more than a year to bring financial order to the union and build a solid base to meet our budgetary needs. Harry Johnson, the division treasurer, had once served in my position in Indonesia, and sympathized with our needs and supported our initiatives.

Soon after we'd arrived in Indonesia, I confirmed that many Church employees were helping themselves to denominational funds. It was an especially sticky problem, since it had been going on so long that it was now viewed as acceptable behavior.

Since embezzling occurred in both government and private enterprise, why should the Church be tight-fisted with its money? Everyone agreed in principle that it was wrong to "steal," but the actual definition of the word had become clouded. The workers sincerely believed that actual stealing required (1) being caught red-handed, and/or (2) taking so much that another person was reduced to poverty.

While traveling in Sumatra to attend a constituency meeting, someone (we'll call him Matthew) asked me how I intended to deal with my associate, who allegedly was embezzling funds. When I replied "nothing," Matthew objected and said I should follow custom and transfer the embezzler to another position. In turn, I assured Matthew that I would do nothing unless it was proven that funds were actually being taken — and that if proven guilty, the person responsible would lose his job.

Matthew said my position was too harsh, since Indonesian workers were poorly compensated and often needed the extra cash. But I challenged him that it was unfair to allow one individual to take funds, at the expense of others and their needs.

Sure enough, I found that not only was my associate pocketing money, but that Matthew himself was submitting duplicate receipts on his expense reports, including one from a payment to the Indonesian Bible Society.

I became suspicious of Matthew's reports and went to the Bible Society to verify the receipts. I was told that one of the receipts was indeed legitimate, but that a Bible Society employee with whom Matthew had promised to share the proceeds had forged the other receipt. When this Bible Society employee (who came from the same ethnic background as Matthew) saw me in the office of the Bible Society treasurer, he suspected that the gig was up, so he took an armed soldier with him to Matthew's house late one night and threatened to kill him if he didn't confess. Matthew did indeed confess, and we accepted his resignation with sadness, for he had served the Church for a number of years.

Later, while auditing accounting records at our mission office in South Borneo, I reviewed expense reports of the treasurer (we'll call him Saney). Saney had reported "miscellaneous expenses," in English, without any supporting documentation, followed by an entry "ongkos lain-lain" (Indonesian for "miscellaneous expenses"), again with no supporting documentation. I was neither deceived nor amused.

Soon we also found that the president of the West Java Mission was selling, for personal gain, pharmaceuticals he was expected to deliver to the Bandung Hospital.

In another coup of detection, we found that the treasurer of our largest local field, the North Sumatra Mission, had personally appropriated tithes and offerings given by a prominent local physician.

Within a span of 60 days we dismissed from Church employ these four top Indonesian officials who had been embezzling funds. My disciplinary authority was being tested, for the union committee had concluded, with full support of division administration, that a strong lesson needed to be delivered. Amazingly, for the next four years in Jakarta, we only had one other embezzlement, this one involving a medical clinic, in which the perpetrator fled to another area of the country to avoid answering for his crime.

But I paid a strong political price. Immediate efforts were made to get rid of me, and a fellow overseas missionary prepared a petition that asked for my termination and urged Indonesians to sign it. But we remained convinced that we had done the right thing, and rode out the storm.

We prepared to take a six-month furlough in 1971. Cheryl was now 10 years old and Sam eight, so we decided to take a global educational tour at our own expense on our return trip home. We spent six weeks touring Europe in a Volvo we picked up in Sweden. From Hamerfest, Norway, and south to the Rock of Gibraltar, we put 11,000 miles on the odometer, and my mother joined us in Dublin for the final leg.

Back in the States, we stopped in at a couple of camp meetings and shared mission stories from the Far East, while visiting relatives and friends. Then we settled down for the remaining two months of furlough near Charlotte's aging mother and father in Boulder, where I studied to take the Certified Public Accountant (CPA) exam in early November.

I had been invited to return as auditor for the Division headquarters in Singapore, so it seemed imperative that I become a full-fledged CPA. But as we prepared to return to the Far East, we found that Singapore was restricting the numbers of foreigners who could work there.

But I pushed forward anyway, sitting for the three-day CPA examination in November, then waiting two more months in Colorado, at the division's request, to see if our appeals for a visa would be honored. By early January 1972, when the visa still had not been approved, I was asked to return alone to the Far East and carry on my new job assignment from South Korea, without a permanent base.

Eventually our visa was approved, but we waited until school was out in May before reuniting in Taipei, as a missionary family. Then we traveled back to Singapore together to make our new home.

Singapore was a former British colony, and there was no language barrier. On the rare occasion when we met someone who could not speak English, we could switch over to Bahasa Indonesia, which is almost identical to Malay. We found Singapore to be clean, safe, well-organized, and very Western. Life was so good, in fact, that sometimes we felt embarrassed to call ourselves "missionaries."

Even so, my new work in auditing was fraught with challenges. I had long felt that denominational accounting was where I was most needed, for no other Protestant denomination had such a vast worldwide organization, and in my travels through the territory, I had found occasional accounting lapses and misappropriated funds. I always tried to be helpful, for I had been exposed to the best in business training and accounting standards, and wanted to pass it on. Now my territory encompassed the Church's Far Eastern Division, from Japan and Korea in the north, south to Indonesia, east to the islands of Micronesia, and west to Thailand.

Then, in 1975, right after Cheryl's graduation from the eighth grade and during the General Conference Quinquennial Session in Vienna, I was invited to transfer to the General Conference office itself (then located in Takoma Park, Maryland) as an associate in the auditing department. Now my service area would encompass the whole world field.

While Charlotte and I were in Vienna for the Church's international business session, Cheryl spent the school vacation with friends in Singapore, and Sam ventured back to Indonesia, where he stayed with a cousin, Charles Tidwell, in Menado, who was the dean at Mount Klabat College, on the northern tip of Sulawesi Island. Charles and his family had spent a lifetime of missionary service in Asia.

We reunited as a family back in Singapore and prepared once again to fold our tent and move on. We had been missionaries for 14 years, and we would miss the excitement of our work in mission lands and the signal feeling of being needed where workers are few. At least once a year we had been able to don our evangelistic hats and conduct successful public crusades in places like Leyte Island in the Philippines, Torajaland in South Sulawesi, and the islands of Sumatra and Borneo. But now we were being asked to give our best back in our homeland. Our aging parents and other family members would be nearby.

Just a year after our return from mission service, Charlotte's mother suffered a cerebral hemorrhage and went to sleep in the Blessed Hope of the resurrection.

Chapter 5:
Reaping What We Had Sown

We saw our new job as an extension of our commitment to the global Church. While Cheryl and Sam were in school, Charlotte served as an administrative secretary in the General Conference, first in risk-management services, then in treasury. Her favorite work in her later years was as treasury's liaison with missionaries under appointment to our former home territory in the Far East. She not only assisted with their travel and shipping arrangements, but gave them firsthand tips about their future work and living conditions.

I felt at home with the auditing staff, treasurers, and other GC officers. Most of our fellow workers had either come to the GC from homes abroad, or had served in mission lands.

My immediate supervisor, a deeply sensitive man named Ralph Davidson, was a highly competent auditor and accountant who dealt kindly with those he saw as committed to the Lord. Unfortunately, job pressures weighed heavily on him, as he prepared for retirement at Annual Council time, in the autumn of 1976.

Annual Council meetings in those days were usually held in the large Takoma Park church, and early one morning I received a call from Clyde Franz, the General Conference Secretary. Would I please come to President Pierson's office for a meeting with the two of them?

They greeted me cordially and informed me that they wanted me to fill the vacancy being left by Davidson, as chief auditor. But even more interesting, I learned that an enabling action had been taken to restructure the Church's internal auditing function, and that, though I was only 38 years old, I would be spearheading that effort. Challenged by the prospects, I accepted and promised to do my best.

The audit function would now be officially known as the Auditing Service and would take on new professionalism. All auditors above the local conference level would become part of the service, and would need to have passed exams qualifying them as certified public accountants (CPAs). At this point I was only one of three CPAs in the North America branch of auditing, and one of only two at headquarters. Our pay would come directly from the General Conference, and in theory we would report directly to the GC Committee. Auditors would hold no administrative responsibility nor serve as members of the Committee itself, but would be invited to its meetings.

We began making these changes, but all too soon Pierson's failing health compelled him to step down as president, and Neal C. Wilson, who had been serving as vice president for the North American Division, took his place.

Wilson took a vastly different approach to presidential leadership than had Pierson. Much less accessible, he tended to arrive at decisions without consultation with his fellow officers, and would bypass board chairmen and departmental directors. He was the author of what we came to call "the presidential style" of leadership. Early on he advised me that on his watch there would be no "cover-ups."

In line with this style, he chose treasury personnel who would readily comply with his views. At the 1980 General Conference Session in Dallas, he succeeded in merging or eliminating several departments. For example, the Youth and Temperance departments were essentially disbanded, at the very time when young people were leaving the Church in droves and problems with alcohol and drugs were on the rise among Church members and in denominational schools. The Sabbath School Department was eliminated, and in my estimation, has led to a general decline in the worldwide Sabbath School program.

During my years overseas I had dealt often with fraud and corruption, and it had been my assumption that in North America, all fraud would be met with swift and open discipline—had not Wilson assured me, after all, that no financial shenanigans would be swept under the rug? But quickly my little balloon of illusion burst, when in rapid succession we had to deal with embezzlement, misappropriation, and incompetent management at the highest levels of Church leadership.

The first of these situations raised its head at Loma Linda University and Medical Center, in California. The institution seemed too big and complex to administer by traditional means, and leaders were hard to recruit, and then often resigned or were moved on quickly. Two extremes in leadership style emerged. Some buried their heads in the sand and avoided raising issues. Others preferred to move precipitously, without seeking broad counsel. In chapters ahead I will deal with the health ministries of the Church in greater detail.

Another example of a mismanagement emerged at the Adventist Media Center, also in California. Adventism has characteristically tended to "tear down its barns to build greater," and has done so at times unnecessarily. This institutional tendency expresses itself as pride in bigness of schools, hospitals, churches, and publishing houses, and allows leadership to hide behind the impressiveness of these facilities, rather than on real accomplishment of the Church's mission.

Wilson developed a concept that successful Church media ministries should be merged into a hugely expensive complex built in Thousand Oaks, California, operated by an additional level of leadership.

This had the effect of distancing ministries such as The Voice of Prophecy, Faith for Today, Breath of Life, and It is Written from their financial supporters, and placed the speaker/directors under the authority of the new center's management and board. In effect this reduced the incentive for the directors to raise funds to support their individual ministries. (Some years later the original complex was sold and a new, slightly downsized base of operations was established in Simi Valley. But from the creation of the Media Center onward, individual ministries have struggled to survive.)

At about this same time, in typical Wilson style, the decision was made to close one of the three publishing houses operated by the Church in North America. Without first studying the Church's overall publishing needs, Wilson determined that the profitable Southern Publishing Association (SPA), then operating in a new facility in suburban Nashville, needed to close. Since word was out by then that to question or oppose Wilson's will was to commit political suicide, the "merging" of SPA with the Review & Herald Publishing Association in Takoma Park took place as planned, and a number of unhappy employees from Tennessee relocated to Maryland.

Appointment of a succession of general managers for the newly created publishing entity followed — usually men with little skill in business management or publishing. These included John Wilkens, a relative of Al McClure and a personal friend of General Vice President Kenneth Mittleider. Wilkens had spent most of his career in denominational treasury work, had never operated a bona fide business, and had no experience in the Church's publishing concerns. Later Harold "Bud" Otis served as president of the Review & Herald, apparently because he had the confidence and friendship of Neal Wilson.

Otis, in particular — who had earlier earned a reputation as a ruthless manager at the Review & Herald — had limited experience in publishing, and during his tenure the publishing house fell into what can only be described as financial shambles. Finally Wilson's own son, Ted, was named Review & Herald president. Ted had no prior publishing or business experience, and left as soon as he was offered a General Conference general vice presidency. After young Wilson's departure, Robert Smith became president — a non-businessman who had worked in the denomination's publishing promotional office. The one exception — the one oasis — in the succession of less-than-inspiring leadership was the short tenure of Bob Kinney as general manager. As a long-term employee, Kinney understood the publishing business and had developed skill and a task-oriented work ethic. He served with distinction.

During the 1980s, Wilson also tuned what he apparently believed were his sensitive business antennae across the nation to Southeastern California and the Church-owned Loma Linda Foods Company. For decades it had served the needs of Seventh-day Adventist vegetarians, who sought protein-rich vegetable-based products to replace animal protein in their diets. More a service than a moneymaker, it came close to breaking even most years and occasionally posted a modest profit.

But Wilson was dissatisfied and turned to Australian health food manufacturers for management assistance. Many years before, the Church in the South Pacific had gained tax exemption from the Australian government for its health-related ministries—including its health food factories that operated under the umbrella trade name "Sanitarium Foods."

The factory had produced and marketed jams, jellies, juices, and cereals—without paying the corporate income taxes required of its competitors. With this striking advantage, it crowded out competitors and relegated such powerful names as Kellogg and Post to also-rans in Australia and New Zealand.

Little wonder, then, that the businessmen from Down Under who Wilson brought in to manage Loma Linda Foods failed miserably. They had no understanding of the American marketplace and its tax laws for Church businesses such as Loma Linda Foods.

Furthermore, those who answered the call to teach the Americans how to turn a profit were not drawn from Australian management's "A-

Team," and during their four years at the helm, the company showed losses of nearly $1 million dollars each year—a staggering reversal.

But Wilson's belief in the economic green thumb of the South Pacific did not waver, and he next turned the management of Loma Linda Foods over to native Australian Eric Feldberg, a former employee at General Conference headquarters. But Feldberg fell ill, and company management was assigned to my long-time friend and financial genius, Alejo Pizarro, Feldberg's former assistant. In short order Pizarro, a Chilean with a Master's of Business Administration (MBA) degree, turned the company around, and for the first time in history, Loma Linda Foods showed a profit for consecutive years, and within three years had nearly paid off its accumulated net operating losses.

But it seemed that the newly profitable status under leadership of a Latin American whom Wilson neither understood nor cared for could not be allowed to stand, and the company was sold to European venture capitalists, without even consulting Pizarro.

The Unions

Yet another example of oversized bureaucracy permeating the entire Church as Wilson took office is known as the "union level" of organization. No one has yet established that unions serve any decidedly worthwhile function for the Church—though each year they consume millions of dollars in tithes and offerings. Still, it seems unlikely that these expensive political centers will be eliminated anytime soon, for union presidents are the most insulated and protected of Church employees. Local conference presidents are key electors in the selection and re-installment of union conference presidents, who in turn are key strategists in helping these presidents retain their offices. The two are mutually interdependent, and in turn union conference presidents have considerable influence over the General Conference president and his officers. As long as union presidents, as a group, support the status quo, this costly arrangement will continue. It's a layer of organization that by the early 1990s came to cost the North American Church nearly $40 million annually, just to meet administrative costs.

Costly Schools

A proliferation of costly secondary schools and colleges also strained Church resources as Wilson came to the fore at the GC. Tradition dictates that every local conference should operate at least one high school (known in Adventism as an "academy") within its geographic area. The tradition also holds that every union needs a college or university in its field.

These costly traditions add significantly to the price of Christian education, placing it well beyond the economic reach of many Adventist families. Adventist colleges, especially, compete tooth and nail for qualified Adventist faculty and break-even enrollments, and with the leveling-off of the baby-boom bulge, Church administrators in the late 1970s were starting to wonder how much longer things could continue this way.

These problems should have been addressed decades before, and by the time I came to the GC, retirement funds were running low, reserves were falling below comfortable levels, and working capital was running short. Later in these pages we will explore the practice of tithing—a great fund-raising success that paradoxically has allowed for institutional inefficiencies.

Davenport Bankruptcy

In 1979, shortly after Wilson took office, the Davenport loan fiasco burst on the Church. From my predecessor, Ralph Davidson, I had learned of the red flags flying over the increasing number of loans being made to Donald Davenport, a physician-turned-real estate magnate. Our fears had grown as Davenport had consistently refused to provide copies of his tax returns or audited financial statements.

Davenport by now was beginning to fall behind in repayment of his obligations, and we had reason to believe he was near bankruptcy. Auditing Service and the Office of General Counsel called for an investigation, which found that for about five years Davenport had been paying interest with new borrowings (technically a Ponzi scheme) and was, in effect, bankrupt. In the bankruptcy scandal that followed, the corporate Church not only suffered the loss of millions of dollars, but surrendered a great deal of spiritual innocence and credibility.

But the Davenport situation was only the beginning of sorrows. Next came the leadership humiliation of Harris Pine Mills. A successful furniture factory that owned valuable forested land in the Pacific Northwest, Harris Pine Mills had been donated to the Church in the 1960s by its founder—yet by 1986, its board voted to file for bankruptcy.

For years I had been urging that Harris Pine be audited—something that historically had never been done at Harris Pine. But Wilson, among others, argued that the GC Auditing Service was inadequate to meet the challenge of such a large commercial audit, and that it would be too costly to engage independent CPAs. The failure to audit the assets and accounting of Harris Pine culminated in its voluntary capitulation—which in turn delivered a devastating hammer-blow to many educational institutions that depended on Harris to provide student labor to pay for educational expenses across the North American Division. But as in the Davenport situation, I believe the loss of credibility cost us far more than the loss of the industry itself.

Often people would tell me, "You don't understand how it is out here, because you work at the General Conference." But I also knew that illicit financial games were being played out right under our noses, at headquarters.

When Lance Butler came from the South Pacific Division to become GC treasurer, he leaned heavily on his under-treasurer, Don Robinson, to deal with issues in North America. In turn, Don's brother, Marvin, ran the East Coast transportation office. While auditing the accounts of the transportation office, we discovered that much of the shipping and packing was being contracted to a company known as Gateway. Further investigation revealed this to be a phantom company in northern Maryland—there was no Gateway office at the given address, only the office of the attorney who had drawn up its legal documents.

It turned out that Gateway had been established solely to funnel business to Marvin Robinson and his work associates, who would check in on Sundays or evenings as employees of Gateway. Then the GC would be invoiced by Gateway for the off-hour work by its own employees—a serious conflict of interest.

We asked for and received Gateway's records and were able to document a list of payments made to GC employees—including a nominal payment to Don Robinson, himself. Things "out there" were apparently not a whole lot different than things "inside the GC."

Another interesting revelation emerged from the offices of ESDA (the name is probably short for "Export SDA"), which made commercial purchases to assist in overseas mission activities. ESDA had been operating for many years at the GC headquarters, and initially served as a purchasing agent for the Church—especially for missionaries in foreign lands or en route to mission service. Erwin Mack, an astute politician with friends in high places, managed ESDA. In our audit one year, we discovered that several hundred dollars worth of camera equipment inventory was missing. We delayed the completion of the inventory count until we could determine what might have happened to the missing stock, and since Mack and his sons were the only ones involved with inventory matters, he was quite sensitive to our questions. I learned that he wanted to submit to a lie-detector test to prove his innocence—and that once he passed the test, he intended to sue me.

He did, in fact, take a polygraph test paid for by the GC, but it revealed only that Mack probably did know what had happened to the missing equipment. I was not sued, though Mack offered no restitution. I still have a copy of that polygraph test report.

As leader of Auditing Service, I was aware that some critics were correctly pointing out that the service should be dissociated from the rest of GC administration. Auditing had traditionally been a part of Treasury, but under our new program, we began answering to the General Conference president.

Ideally, our Auditing Service should have been cut free from all internal influences—including those of both president and treasurer. Though this problem was never fully resolved, I do not believe it compromised our work directly. We retained our friendships and working relationships, while reporting as we deemed necessary. Perhaps our greatest natural enemies were the North American unions. Their presidents inherently seemed to feel that they should not be subjected to constraint and accountability questions.

Another dilemma arose on the question of whether auditors should be appointed or elected. The Auditing Service director and his associate directors were elected at General Conference Session. I was re-elected at the 1980 GC session in Dallas, and again at the 1985 session in New Orleans. Each time, some voiced opposition to my re-election. In 1980 my main detractor was a former friend, the late Ellsworth Reile, then president of the Mid-America Union and a heavily committed business partner of Dr. Davenport.

He was particularly aggrieved by the independence of auditing and wanted greater union-level control of Auditing Service, but I was re-elected over his objections. Again, in New Orleans, some voices called for change, but I felt certain God had called me to this post and that He would let me know when it was time to step down. Often I'd quip, "Many want the auditor removed, but no one wants his job." I represented changes in Auditing Service that bothered many administrators. As an agent for change in a most sensitive area of Church policy, my voice was becoming increasingly unpopular.

Chapter 6:

Driving Nails in My Coffin

Our mandate called on us to recruit young CPAs into Auditing Service, but we faced stiff competition for those bright young people from the Adventist Health System. At the 1988 Spring Meeting, Neal Wilson polished his appeal among union presidents and hospital administrators by urging removal of salary caps for Adventist Health executives.

After the motion eventually passed, I weighed in on the question with an open letter to Wilson, dated April 17, 1989, which reads in part, "It did seem strange that after admitting to serious financial failures and mounting debt far beyond accepted norms in the United States, these leaders should now ask for higher pay. Few businessmen could ever accept the assumption that if a manager is ineffective while earning an annual salary of $75,000 he will somehow be successful if his salary is raised to $140,000."

I objected to both the position and the political processes used to advance the recommendation to a final vote: "It seemed to me that the democratic process was not taken very seriously... . I find it hard to understand why a vote was not taken at the conclusion of the day-long discussion on Wednesday. Instead, you recommended and moved that the motion be tabled. Then late Thursday, the matter was brought back for consideration after much of the opposition had disappeared.... This is not the first time delays, tabling, straw votes, and similar strategies have been used in our convocations to push through an unpopular recommendation."

When my letter circulated, Wilson demanded that I retract it. I told him that if he could identify any inaccuracies in the letter, I would happily do so. Since he seemed unable to identify any misinformation in my four-page manifesto, I declined to take back anything I had written. Our conversation ended when he invited me to pray with him, and we agreed to put the matter behind us.

To illustrate the urgency of my concerns, a short time later I sat in meetings at Loma Linda University, where Medical Center employees with equal or fewer qualifications were receiving salaries three times those earned by their peers at the Foundation or University. CPAs recruited for Auditing Service continued to be tempted away by offers from the health system.

Even so, I knew any popularity I may have once enjoyed was on the wane, for I had lost the support of the union presidents. I had reason to believe that they saw my letter to Wilson as a swipe at them, for I knew they were getting nice perks for their involvement in the health system, and many, indeed, served as chairmen of the health system's boards. The health system was pampering them with freebie cruises to Alaska and other significant gifts, and in turn the hospital administrators were using the union presidents' influence and support to gain their desired ends.

The years rolled by, and it was now my fifteenth year at the General Conference. The 1990 GC Session at the Hoosier Dome in Indianapolis opened (coincidently) on Neal Wilson's 70th birthday. Friends had urged him to step down as president, but he had replied that retiring was "not biblical," and that "once you have put your hand to the plow you can't look back."

But the Nominating Committee did see a need for change, and did not resubmit the name of the aging Wilson as president, opting finally in favor of the youthful and flamboyant Robert S. Folkenberg.

Three days later I was summoned to the new president's suite in the press section of the upper decks of the Dome. Folkenberg came right to the point, advising me that there were "hard-hitting" objections to my re-election as head auditor. He wanted to know if I would prefer to resign rather than face being forced out. I told him I had not come to Indianapolis to resign, but that I recognized that things had changed and that Auditing Service was organizationally supervised by the office of the president. So, I asked him point blank, did he want me to step aside?

He assured me it would be his privilege to work with me, if I were re-elected, so I asked him to allow me to stand for re-election with a "fair vote," and to this we agreed. While the interpretation of "fair" may vary, I felt a simple up or down vote, without Folkenberg's interference, would suffice.

Late Thursday evening Folkenberg and Des Hills, the new chairman of the Nominating Committee, asked me to meet with them. They told me that because of the open letter I had written to Neal Wilson a year earlier, I had not been re-nominated. Folkenberg emphasized the importance of the letter and seemed to be asking me to bow in great tears of repentance. I responded with all honesty that if I had it to do over, I would again write the letter.

The next morning, when the Nominating Committee report was read to the delegates, objections were raised and the nomination of head auditor was referred back to the committee. I heard later that more than 30 individuals testified before the Nominating Committee, and that one said that failing to reappoint me was "like shooting the watchdog" for doing his job.

The issue generated such a furor that the committee reversed itself and I was re-nominated. Cheers erupted from the floor when the constituent assembly voted me back into office.

I'm sure Folkenberg felt singed by this early political defeat, but he remained outwardly cordial. At the time I did not realize the true extent of the efforts he had put forward to have me replaced, and we all returned to suburban Maryland to resume our work.

Only later, while I was on a special assignment in Uganda dealing with ADRA auditing issues, did I learn from a member of the Nominating Committee that I had not actually received the "fair vote" Folkenberg had promised me. Folkenberg was quoted as having said that in publishing the letter, I had committed an "ethical transgression."

When his words were translated into other languages for the benefit of those who did not speak English, however, he appeared to have said that I was guilty of a "moral transgression." Little wonder why after the initial vote, several friends from South America and from Asia put their arms around me in tears.

When I returned to headquarters from Uganda, I went immediately to Folkenberg and asked him why he had broken his word, but he refused to either acknowledge or explain his behavior. I concluded that Folkenberg was not driven by a fully developed sense of honesty.

But I now knew that my future at the GC was tenuous, and I suspected that I had become a marked man. Folkenberg placed the Auditing Service under a vice president, and we were told to communicate with the president only through this intermediary. Wilson had been very selective in extending the royal scepter of access, but Folkenberg was putting it in cold storage. Colleagues warned me that this administrative move could imperil the independence of Auditing, and we soon learned that we had lost all presidential support to do what needed to be done.

My state of grace suffered yet another blow less than a year after Indianapolis. While members of my staff were doing routine auditing at the Columbia Union office, we discovered that a $150,000 "interest-free" home loan had been extended to the newly elected vice president for North America, Alfred McClure, Folkenberg's long-time close personal friend.

Further investigation revealed that money receipted to the "worthy-student fund" had been used to provide salaries for both Folkenberg and McClure's wives, though they were doing no work to justify the pay. What a predicament! Should I go against my conscience and professional ethics and sweep the matter under the rug, or risk my future by embarrassing arguably the two most powerful leaders of the World Church?

I thought of Daniel, facing the threat of the lions. He could have closed his windows during his midday meditations. Now, the temptation arose to take the easy road and brush off the irregularity with the words "not considered material." In the end, conscience would not allow me to cover up what was happening. I believed God had called me to this assignment to stand firm at moments such as these.

I sought counsel from the large accounting firm, Ernst and Young, and for a fee of $600 asked this public firm to write the disclosures for the Columbia Union financial statements. When our report was published, phone calls immediately began coming in, including one from a chastened and tearful McClure, who told me that this was the first such wrong he had ever committed. He begged me to alter the report, while conveniently failing to apprise me that he had just sold his personal residence in Georgia for greater than market value to the health system, whose board he chaired.

As it turned out, the money-laundering scheme involving the two presidential wives apparently originated with Ronald Wisbey, then Columbia Union president. Wisbey had taken an adversarial position toward me during the Davenport era, when he had supported the investment of personal and Church funds in the doctor's post office properties. To channel funds to the presidents' wives, Wisbey had approached the GC treasurer, Don Gilbert (considered a man of impeccable moral discernment) and had tried to convince him to launder these large donations through the GC. Wisbey, who had competed politically with McClure for the VP position, now wanted to show his charity in defeat by helping the new presidents, who would be living within his union territory—an area conceded to have a particularly high cost of living. Gilbert had refused to involve the GC treasury in the plan, so Wisbey slipped the funds through his own union's accounts, instead.

Wisbey tried to convince me to modify our audit report, and when this failed, he invited me to meet with a rather large delegation (Church employees, primarily) to hear their reasons why the report should be altered. The group literally booed me when I pointed out that this was not an auditors' problem, but a question of Church leaders' integrity, and I quoted Ellen White's statement that our "transactions should be as transparent as the sunlight."

Meanwhile, as a retired senior statesman for the Church, Neal Wilson counseled Folkenberg and McClure to write letters asking that the unearned salaries given to their wives be discontinued. But they made no apologies and recognized no wrongdoing. Folkenberg was known to be skilled in the art of retaliation, and I knew my day would soon come.

By 1994, preparations were well in hand for the 56th Session of the World Church in The Netherlands, and I knew that every effort would be made to force me from office before then. Just how this would be arranged I did not know—but my time was running out.

Chapter 7:
Challenges of the Right Arm

Ellen White writes extensively about the Church's health-care ministry, emphasizing its importance by calling it the "right arm of the message." But during the very earliest stages of my responsibilities at the General Conference (GC), I saw that the denomination faced challenges from this "right arm," especially at Loma Linda University Medical Center (LLUMC). Our department was assigned financial vigil over this monolith, and I quickly saw that internal controls at LLUMC had been giving way to personal politics.

For example, in years before Neal Wilson became General Conference president (prior to and including most of 1978), he chaired the Loma Linda University (LLU) Board of Trustees, while David B. Hinshaw, Sr., was dean of the School of Medicine.

In the early 1970s, Lynn Hilde, an LLU 1971 graduate, was taking a surgical residency at LLUMC and was caught moonlighting, contrary to hospital policy. So Hinshaw suspended Hilde from the surgical residency program.

Hilde, however, was aware that other LLUMC surgical residents were being rotated to a hospital in Blythe, California, on weekends, to supplement their hospital salaries. So Hilde sought legal counsel, and the law firm he retained discovered that, in fact, an independent company, University Medical Group, Inc., was contracting with the Blythe Hospital for the residents' services. And surprise! The company was owned by David B. Hinshaw, Sr.; C. Victor (Dick) Way, LLUMC Administrator; Tom Zirkle, Jr.; and other senior members of the Surgery Department.

This company also had contracted with LLUMC and Riverside County Hospital to provide surgical gloves, and Hilde exposed this self-serving conflict of interest to Wilson. Hilde was reinstated in the surgical residency program—and he, in turn, dropped his legal action.

But gross improprieties continued. On April 3, 1975, Way and Hinshaw made a down payment of $52,000 toward joint ownership of Lakeview, a $525,000, 2,073-acre ranch in Lake County, Oregon. At about that same time, a member of the radiology faculty practice group sued the radiology department for financial impropriety. An audit in the discovery phase of the suit revealed, rather serendipitously, that Way had misappropriated more than $916,000, some diverted from university accounts with checks co-signed by him and Hinshaw.

Later in 1975 Robert Pierson (then GC president); Wilson (then GC vice president for North America); and Willis Hackett (a GC general vice president) repeatedly discussed among themselves what to do about the $916,000 misappropriation and other evidences of financial impropriety. But according to Robert Warren, an attorney with the firm of Gibson Dunn and Crutcher, not until May 1977 did Wilson tell the Board of Trustees about the problem. In January 1978 Hinshaw resigned under pressure, though he denied any involvement in, or knowledge of, the misappropriation of funds. This denial came in the face of Wilson's statement that Hinshaw had indeed co-signed checks with Way as payment to Way's private enterprises. Yet Wilson defended Hinshaw's innocence, saying that Hinshaw had simply signed blank checks when he left town so that Way could carry on medical center business in his absence. In Wilson's eyes, Hinshaw's only apparent sin was that he had trusted Way.

The Board of Trustees, under Wilson's leadership, did not file criminal charges against either Hinshaw or Way, and on February 24, 1978, Way signed an Agreement of Restitution to repay the University $916,000.

The ranch in Oregon became the focus of LLU's recovery efforts, though Way and Hinshaw had very little equity in it. LLU proposed a plan that would allow Way to make a profit on the sale of the land and use that money to repay his debt to the University. Although "innocent," Hinshaw and his wife signed an agreement with LLU on March 4, 1980, in which he agreed "to assist Way in fulfilling his obligations to the University, and to settle all disputes between Hinshaw and the University."

As it turned out, Way and Hinshaw were unsuccessful in whatever efforts they made to refinance the ranch property. Nine months later, on December 9, 1980, the University "released and forever discharged Hinshaw's liability for the actions of Way," in exchange for his agreement to "execute any and all documents" that would enable the University to sell the ranch to a third party.

On February 4, 1981, the property was sold to J. R. Ferguson & Associates, Inc., who also assumed a $200,000 promissory note obligation to LLU. By August 1983, however, Ferguson was delinquent on the $200,000 second trust deed-promissory note, and the $500,000 first deed of trust was in default to Downey Savings & Loan.

Subsequently Downey named LLU a defendant in a suit over the ranch default. On November 10, 1987, the LLU investment management committee voted that the Lakeview property be sold for $25,000 cash, provided that LLU be dismissed as a defendant from Downey's suit, with prejudice. Of the original $916,180 misappropriated, LLU recovered only $98,978, so even if the question of lost interest is ignored, LLU still lost $835,202. Why the board, under Wilson's chairmanship, did not deal more resolutely with this issue is not clear, but it has led to serious speculation of impropriety.

In yet another enterprise, in his capacity as a LLUMC administrator, Way served as chief financial officer of Electronic Data Processing (EDP), which served the separate clinical practice corporations at LLUMC. Cleverly, Way had transferred computer operations offsite to a garage and began to publicly market EDP services under the business name Desert Systems, thus allowing him to personally appropriate sums of money for services, while using LLUMC's equipment and capital.

At about this time, the Radiology Department, led by Melvin Judkins, M.D., established a Chairman's Fund to finance research, teaching, and new equipment by withholding 10 percent of the teaching faculty members' salaries. The faculty did not object to this system, but some believed that the use of these funds should be disclosed to the radiology faculty. Disclosure was denied, so a faculty member of the Department of Radiology brought a legal complaint against the Department of Radiology and LLUMC. For the discovery phase the physician engaged an outside CPA to investigate the financial records, with the assistance of GC auditors.

The scheme finally unraveled when it was found that Way had developed an elaborate plan to embezzle large sums of money. It worked like this. Let's say that Radiology asks for equipment with a price tag of $1 million, and Way in turn asks Radiology for a $50,000 voluntary contribution toward the purchase. Way then goes to the Board of Trustees and asks for authorization to purchase the equipment for $1 million. Unknown to the chairman of Radiology or the Board of Trustees, Way transfers the $50,000 from one university trust entity to another, until it finally ends up in one of his own personal corporations. One auditor involved in the investigation stated that Way "admitted to everything that was proven against him."

In concept this kind of behavior is what ruined Enron 30 years later. LLUMC was simply ahead of its time. Separate corporate entities were being established to hide questionable dealings from the Board and the General Conference. It was not enough that LLUMC already had three administrative heads: (1) the University, (2) the Medical Center, and (3) the Foundation. These new and creative entities included Universal Health Care, Inc. (UHCI), established around February 1980 for the operation of Learjet aircraft to provide long-range air transportation for the newly developed ambulatory surgery center.

The vice president for Medical Affairs, Marlowe Schaffner, a highly respected, long-time former missionary physician in Africa, commissioned an officer of the group, Kenneth Dortch, to study the feasibility of the Learjet project.

Negotiations opened with Miller & Schroeder, a lending company, to obtain financing to the tune of $4 million. Little is known of the company, but Steven W. Erickson, a senior vice president, readily acknowledges that UHCI was corporately separate from the Seventh-day Adventist Church and LLUMC, but that he believed the Church had a moral and legal obligation to restore the funds in case of default. The wording of the promissory note specifically states that LLUMC "guarantees" or "cosigns" the note.

When the project failed, the CPA firm of Laventhol & Horwath was engaged to sort out the financial mess, and it found the accounting records in such a state of disarray as to preclude the full completion of the assignment. For example, incomplete flight logs revealed that of more than 180 logged flights, at most two were related to the stated purpose of the corporation. The rest included such trivial business as a flight to Reno, Nevada, to buy fishing tackle. LLUMC and the General Conference once again had to come to an embarrassing rescue.

Conflicts of interest have been so common at Loma Linda over the years as to become nearly routine. For example, LLUMC has widely marketed its Proton Beam Accelerator (PBA) services, a high tech cancer-treatment device. James M. Slater chaired the Department of Radiation Oncology (which offers PBA services). His son, Jerry D. Slater, also a radiation oncologist and department member, succeeded him as department chairman, and another son, James B. Slater, Ph.D., was also a member of the Radiation Oncology Department.

PBA cancer treatment at LLUMC began in 1990, when a team of scientists and technicians created a Radiation Research Laboratory (Rad Lab). Jon W. Slater, yet another son of James Slater, was an early hire on the team. He had a BS degree in computer science and was involved in the design of the facility and in assembling the engineering team to maintain it. The first patient was treated in October 1990.

Then, in 1993, Jon Slater formed Optivus Technology, Inc., and hired away the entire Rad Lab team already recruited and employed by the Loma Linda University Medical Center. These 44 employees, 37 of whom were engineers or technical support personnel, were apportioned 20 percent of the fledgling company, and Jon Slater retained the other 80 percent.

At this writing, Optivus has 75 employees, and the company retains exclusive rights to the most comprehensive intellectual property portfolio in the proton therapy industry. In 1998 Jon Slater founded PerMedics, Inc., to create PC-based software solutions for proton beam therapy, as well as for conventional radiation therapy.

I highlight this case of nepotism to show how often transactions occur at less than arm's length. Terms of Slater's contract with the Loma Linda Medical Center are held in secrecy; however, it seems significant that Jon W. Slater did not come to LLUMC as a functioning company, able to prove that his firm possessed superior technical ability to support the PBA. Rather, through family connections, he was able to take over an existing technical service team — clearly a win-win deal for the Slater family!

Chapter 8:
A Legal Challenge for Loma Linda University

The case of Stewart W. Shankel and George M. Grames at Loma Linda University (LLU) evolved shortly before my termination as director of the GC Auditing Service. Reviewing their situation here illustrates the style of administration often found in Adventist institutions and mirrors my own experience.

Both Shankel and Grames were nephrologists and professors of medicine, who had served on the faculty of the School of Medicine for more than 20 years. Shankel, whose brother Clinton was president of the West Indonesia Union when I was treasurer, chaired the department of medicine in the School of Medicine and was instrumental in recruiting Neal Bricker to LLU. Bricker is a distinguished research nephrologist, who had served as chairman of the departments of medicine or sections of nephrology at several major U.S. universities. He rose to prominence in nephrology circles and served as president of the American Society of Nephrology and treasurer of the International Society of Nephrology for 17 years. One of Bricker's major research endeavors was to identify the natriuretic hormone (NH), in which he had invested the previous

25 years of his career, before coming to LLU. His goal was to identify, synthesize, and market this substance, which could revolutionize the diuretic market, because it does not induce potassium excretion, a major disadvantage of other potent diuretics.

When he arrived at LLU, he did not yet have a patent on the isolation method, but a short time later, he did sign over his rights to an anticipated patent to LLU, with the understanding that the institution would support his research, until he found a pharmaceutical company as a joint partner. One such company was Boots Pharmaceutical Company, represented by William Wechter, a Ph.D. in chemistry. Wechter was so impressed with the project that he resigned from Boots and joined Bricker in his efforts to isolate NH. So Bricker added Wechter's name to the patent application, because of his potential role in identifying the chemical structure of NH.

After a year of seemingly harmonious collaboration, Wechter and Bricker appear to have had a falling-out, and Wechter met privately with Hinshaw who, after leaving as dean of the School of Medicine, had returned to LLU as vice president for medical affairs. What was planned in private is not known, but subsequent events leave little to the imagination.

After this meeting, Wechter no longer reported to either Shankel or Bricker, but to Hinshaw, and Bricker's laboratory was closed and he was told to leave LLU, with six months termination pay — however, LLU would still retain the patent rights to NH. Shankel remained very supportive of Bricker, and on February 14 (Valentine's Day), 1991, Shankel was fired as chairman of the department of medicine.

During this same time a Dr. Ronald Billing, a Ph.D. researcher, had been recruited from UCLA by the immunology laboratory of the department of surgery. At UCLA he had developed a monoclonal antibody (CBL-1) that was apparently effective in treating transplant rejection as well as certain immunological central nervous system diseases and cancers. But Billing apparently suffered from emotional problems, and was abruptly terminated by the surgery department. Even more egregious than his precipitous termination was the apparent theft of his antibody by the LLU immunology laboratory. This was accomplished by announcing, soon after Billing's departure, the discovery of a "new" monoclonal antibody, which was named "DBH" (Hinshaw's initials). They continued to treat the same patients with this "new" antibody, with no change in protocol or Institutional Review Board approval.

These two cases prompted 19 faculty members to sign a letter to the Board of Trustees, dated August 8, 1990. The letter was critical of the medical school's administration and asked for an investigation into the allegations of theft of proprietary research. The Board of Trustees had no apparent interest in investigating allegations of theft and came to the immediate defense of the administration, and the question even arose as to whether the 19 faculty members who had signed the letter should be allowed to remain at LLU.

The administration was aware that Shankel and Grames were primarily responsible for the letter, but also knew that they could not terminate their employment with the department of medicine, since they were compensated by a separate practice corporation (a requirement for employment was a faculty appointment in the School of Medicine). So Lynn

Lynn Behrens, then recently appointed chair of the School of Medicine, revoked the faculty appointments to the School of Medicine of Shankel, Grames, and Lysle W. Williams. (Though Dr. Williams had not signed the letter, he was known to be very supportive of Shankel, as attested by critical letters he had written earlier to the Board of Trustees).

These precipitous terminations were reported to the American Association of University Professors (AAUP), and Jordan E. Kurland, AAUP associate general secretary, began exchanging letters with Behrens. In an August 23, 1991, letter Behrens wrote in reference to the 1958 Statement on Procedural Standards in Faculty Dismissal Proceedings (adopted jointly by AAUP and the Association of American Colleges), arguing: "The standards appear to have been drafted for a general application in higher education, but clearly do not meet the specific challenges and standards of a medical school involving clinical employment and compensation. There are also unique issues presented by the close relationship to the Seventh-day Adventist Church and its mission which are not addressed by the guidelines."

In a reply, dated August 27, the associate general secretary replied: "On the contrary, these standards are deemed by their framers to apply to, and indeed are in force in the large preponderance of medical schools and their clinical faculties.... The procedural standards have always been considered to be equally applicable at Church-related colleges and universities, and we are not aware of what there is about Loma Linda University's church relationship that would justify not affording fundamental Safeguards of academic due process."

An onsite investigation was planned by the AAUP, but the by-now President Behrens denied access to the campus and prohibited LLU administration from testifying at the investigative hearings, held at the Hilton Hotel in San Bernardino. The investigators were Ralph S. Brown (Law), of Yale University, and Samuel F. Bessman (Pediatrics and Pharmacology), of the University of Southern California. The investigation concluded that "the administration of Loma Linda University acted in violation of the 1940 Statement of Principles on Academic Freedom and Tenure and in disregard of the 1958 Statement on Procedural Standards in Faculty Dismissal Proceedings in dismissing Professors Stewart W. Shankel and George M. Grames and Lysle W. Williams, Jr., without first having demonstrated adequate cause for dismissal in an adjudicative hearing of record before an elected faculty body. The hearing procedure offered to the three professors denied them basic safeguards of academic due process by not being available until after the dismissals were effected and by placing the burden on the professors to prove that the administration erred in dismissing them."

The complete investigative report was published in the May-June, 1992 issue of Academe (www.aaup.org). As can be imagined, LLU administration was placed on the AAUP's censure list, published in each issue of Academe.

Drs. Shankel and Grames subsequently filed a claim with the National Labor Relations Board (NLRB). However, the Board refused to take the case on the basis of the First Amendment prohibition for entanglement between church and state, the same basis invoked in my lawsuit a few years later.

Drs. Shankel and Grames then filed a civil lawsuit claiming wrongful discharge as "whistleblowers."

The lawsuit was again defended by claiming separation of church and state and ecclesiastical privilege. Drs. Shankel and Grames' requirements for settlement remained the same throughout the entire litigation process — namely, reinstatement of their faculty appointments, a letter of explanation to the alumni and faculty of the School of Medicine, and an independent investigation into the allegations of theft of proprietary research.

After eight years of LLU's numerous stalling tactics, the judge finally set a trial date. LLU requested settlement on the same day. The investigation into the allegations of theft of proprietary research, which was an integral component of the settlement agreement, was conducted by retired Judge H. Lee Sarokin, US Court of Appeals. The report exonerated LLU on all counts.

Regarding Bricker, Judge Sarokin wrote, "At about the same time, a grievance proceeding was initiated by Dr. Bricker against the University. Dr. Shankel agreed to recuse himself from the grievance proceeding and appointed a committee from the Department of Medicine." However, the judge neglected to include the committee's findings, dated December 26, 1989, in his report: "As we have reviewed the material, particularly Bricker's direct communications with the Vice-President for Medical Affairs, a recurring theme has emerged. The Vice-President for Medical Affairs institutes programs, supports individuals, and is involved with operational details without apparently going through the established 'chain of command.' This insistence on personal and financial control that bypasses the Dean, Department Chairman, Section Chief, and Laboratory Director is a very divisive style of management that is bound, as this case has illustrated, to have disruptive effects far beyond the individuals in a particular laboratory or project."

Judge Sarokin continued, "There is little doubt that the administration permitted Dr. Wechter to take control of the subject research as the result of the controversy between him and Dr. Bricker, but that decision, whether justified or not, was to further the project, not to deprive Dr. Bricker of whatever proprietary rights he had in the natriuretic hormone research project."

Unfortunately, this statement by Judge Sarokin does not square with the facts. Prior to Bricker's grievance, Shankel attended a six-hour meeting with Bricker and LLU administration, with their legal counsel. The administration never deviated from its position that Bricker be terminated and that LLU would retain the patent rights to NH. Further, during the subsequent grievance proceedings, LLU was actively pursuing an application to the US Patent Office for a patent on the hormone. The application was rejected by the patent office and twice revised by Wechter and resubmitted, without Bricker's knowledge or input. Both revisions were rejected, the last toward the end of the grievance hearings. On the last day of the hearing Hinshaw informed the committee that there was no patent. He then said, "It was elected to return any rights whatsoever that the institution had in various forms — or that Dr. Wechter has — returned all these rights to Dr. Bricker."

A committee member asked, "Why were the patents turned down by the patent office?" Wechter responded, "It's a little more than just turned down. In this particular case, they have disallowed on two occasions now all claims. And the reasons why they have disallowed them are many, but the basic reason is that they don't believe that it's an adequate description. In other words, if you took the patent, you should be able to isolate and make natriuretic hormone. And in this particular circumstance, the patent office — and at this date, I agree with them — says that it is not enabling."

Thus, Hinshaw believed that he was merely returning worthless patent rights to Bricker. Although the patent was not enabling, Wechter continued to search for NH and presented a display of his research at the 1993 Alumni Postgraduate Convention. But in light of Wechter's remarks to the grievance committee, it does seem curious that, within months of having the patent rights returned to him, Bricker was indeed able to obtain a patent on the isolation of NH from the United States Patent Office, #5106630. Now, 15 years later, Bricker and Shankel have indeed isolated, identified, and synthesized NH.

Both Bricker and Shankel joined the faculty of the University of California at Riverside (UCR). Not only have they made great progress in the identification and synthesis of natriuretic hormone, Shankel was asked to develop a plan for a four-year medical school and present it to administration. Shankel's plan was unorthodox, in that it called for a $100 million dollar research institute, but no university hospital. Nonetheless, it was accepted by the chancellor and ultimately by the Board of Regents of the University of California. A medical school at UCR will become a reality in the near future.

The loss to Loma Linda University has been incalculable. Besides the millions of dollars spent in the defense of Shankel and Grames' legal action, disenchantment of recently graduated alumni at the treatment of two of their most admired professors resulted in a marked drop in contributions to the university and its affiliated organizations. The greatest loss, however, has been the departure of the "best and brightest" teachers, clinicians, and researchers from the department of medicine, considered the "backbone" of any medical school. Loma Linda University settled its legal challenge and was exonerated by an independent investigation. But it lost far more than money and personnel. It may have lost its heart and soul.

Chapter 9:

Blue Duck Business

The Adventist Church has grown large, using a hierarchical organizational style with considerable power at the top, consisting of the president, his underlings, and the influential union presidents. Neal Wilson perfected this system, and came to believe that he possessed the kind of administrative genius that deserved a strengthened presidential position. He left this legacy of power to his successor, Robert Folkenberg.

Though Adventists generally understand and sometimes complain about the excess of power at the top, the status quo remains effectively unchallenged, and voices for change are muted.

During his tenure, Wilson cut back many of the departments that had once had the greatest impact on local congregations—Youth, Temperance, and Sabbath School. He closed, sold, or bankrupted institutions such as Southern Publishing Association, Loma Linda Foods, and Harris Pine Mills, and as Wilson's successor, Robert Folkenberg continued the tradition.

For example, he called on an old business associate, Andrews University faculty member Duane McBride, to perform a governance study that would have the effect of further enhancing the power and influence of the presidential office.

When Folkenberg—high-flying missionary pilot, gifted bilingual preacher, and businessman—took the helm of Church leadership, he was determined, among other things, to address the problems of literature evangelism in the Church. He had stated his concerns about the program often, believing that it consumed an inordinate portion of the Church's tithe dollar—about 3 percent.

At that time, the sales-management arm of the colporteur ministry was the Home Health Education Service (HHES), which ordered books from the Review & Herald or Pacific Press, then administered their distribution by literature evangelists to their clients. It also extended credit to the colporteurs' customers and recruited, trained, and gave continuing education to the colporteur workforce. By and large it helped preserve the Church's institutional colporteur program for many years, though it generally ran at a deficit and failed to show the kind of year-to-year growth administrators would have liked. All agreed that the HHES program needed to become more effective, and earnest efforts were made during the 1970s and 1980s (during some very tough economic times) to bring the program back up to speed.

HHES generally ran at a deficit—and this deficit was covered by tithe funds, at a rate of about 3 percent of tithe a year. I myself had served as a literature evangelist during a highly productive and educational summer vacation from college, so I was especially hurt when the North

American Division in the early days of Folkenberg's administration voted to shut down the HHES and withdraw from the business of promoting door-to-door sale of literature. This work would now be left entirely in the hands of the publishing houses—at their option.

Another of Folkenberg's business associates, the late Al McClure, had encouraged the idea of tapping the services of former Review and Herald president Harold F. "Bud" Otis, who had convinced McClure and others that he could direct a self-sustaining book-sales program that would not require Church subsidies. Otis was keen on developing and marketing Bible story videos, which he believed would garner huge profits. While I believe HHES could have been massaged into a cost-efficient operation (given the improving economy and the growing Hispanic appetite in the United States for bilingual materials), instead an entirely new company, Family Enrichment Resources (FER), was established to sell the as-yet non-existent videos. Three union presidents supported McClure in the plan, and Otis was installed as president.

Unfortunately, many political debts were being paid after the musical chairs in leadership at the 1990 Indianapolis General Conference Session, and it appears that Otis was given his new assignment in lieu of the position he lost as a liaison in the new Church division in Russia. The post in Russia had come to Otis, compliments of his close friendship with Wilson, and Otis appears to have lost the post in part because a significant lay donor became dissatisfied with his stewardship. Another complicating factor was the need to make way for Wilson's son, Ted, to become a Division president—preferably one with close ties to movers and shakers in North America.

Five years before, when I had asked certain Church leaders why Otis, who was then president of the Review & Herald, was asked to become involved in the closing of Harris Pine Mills, I was told that his chief attribute was ruthlessness. Perhaps trading on this trait, Otis was entrusted with the creation of the new FER publishing program.

Otis was smooth of speech and able to take advantage of permissive, new division policies to convince the Pacific, Atlantic, and Columbia unions to consolidate their sales under FER.

But interestingly enough, two conferences in each of the Atlantic and Columbia unions declined to join the new program, and the other five NAD unions opted out entirely. In the three supporting unions, however, what can only be described as a hostile takeover occurred, with the firing of publishing sales leadership and their replacement with Otis's personnel. FER began operations in January 1992.

FER proceeded to sign a contract with a marketing firm, Blue Duck, to produce and market the promised animated videos. It is not known whether Blue Duck had previously produced any such products, but I do know that over a period of time, FER showed payments of $370,000 to this firm, but had only one script and a production and marketing plan to show for it.

Otis was determined, however, to produce and market a Disneylike, three-part video series on the story of creation, the life of Jesus, the Book of Acts, and the prophecies of Revelation, and FER needed additional funding. At a January 5, 1996, meeting of the FER board, Blue Duck made a presentation regarding a possible source of funding. This plan called for placing between $2.4 to 2.6 million on a "no risk" hold in a bank.

Through a complex international banking scheme (this was the 1990s, and anything was possible in venture capitalization!), this money would then magically generate the $15 million needed to produce the videos! Dru Cox and a heretofore unknown investor going by the improbable name of Gary Ferry then agreed to place $2 million in a reserve to advertise the videos. The board authorized Otis to pursue funding, but asked that the proposal first be approved by the FER attorney — since Blue Duck was a marketing company, not a financial consulting firm. Otis neglected to seek this legal counsel, but continued to pursue the funding through a Canadian investor, and he and FER treasurer, Reginald Frood, traveled to Toronto and met with Tom Tiffin, the investor, at the Bank of Nova Scotia. They came away "convinced of the feasibility of the plan."

Aware that the FER board action did not allow the company to place any money at risk, FER officers asked the Columbia Union to place $2.4 million in an account controlled by FER and the union association. When it became clear that doing so would place Columbia Union funds at risk, however, the union officers declined to do so.

The investor in Canada was said to be "very upset," but claimed to have enough faith in the overall project to put together a private group of investors who would allow profits from the joint investment to go to the video project. This proposal sounded too good to be true, and sure enough, the investor informed Otis that expenses would be incurred. So on April 24, 1996, Otis asked Ralph Martin, then Columbia Union president, and Don Russell, then Columbia Union treasurer, for an immediate advance on FER's subsidy to cover the payment the investor was requesting. On that same day, $50,000 was wired to the investor in Canada, without the approval of the Union Executive Committee.

Several days later, Harold Lee, then Columbia Union secretary, became involved, and the three officers authorized a $300,000 advance from union operating funds, again without Executive Committee approval. The money was released to FER as an interest-bearing line of credit. The loan agreement was signed by Otis and Frood. But neither the FER finance committee's nor the Columbia Union board's approval was sought. Otis simply assured the officers that any money sent to Canada would be returned within 10 weeks and would yield millions of dollars of profit. Martin, Russell, and Lee believed that if FER failed to repay any part of the $300,000, the union would simply withhold future subsidies until the debt was repaid. Martin, in fact, chaired the FER Board of Trustees, and Don Russell served as a board member. But inexplicably these men who served on both boards seemed ignorant of the fact that all FER subsidies bypassed the union altogether! The argument that the unauthorized line of credit was secured by future subsidies, therefore, had no merit.

Otis asked that the electronic transfers to Canada be made through the union treasury, and thus between April 24 and June 11, 1996, four payments totaling $363,000 were wired to Nissi Financial Corporation, the off-shore investment company supposedly run by the Canadian investor. An additional $60,000 was wired directly from FER.

Such risky financial contortions spoke volumes about these men's overall business judgment, but Otis in particular seemed to enjoy Folkenberg's absolute confidence. In his "From the GC President" newsletter of December 1995, Folkenberg boasted about the success of this "innovative new method to expand sales….more effectively," by privatizing the Church's publishing program as Family Enrichment Resources.

As things began to come to a head in 1996, FER had had four years to prove itself. I had been thrown out of office about 12 months before the GC president pronounced FER a success. Folkenberg outlined the major cost savings during the previous four years in these words: "During the last four years the three unions…saved a total of $6,695,199 in addition to not paying for publishing directors, secretaries, office expenses and related programs. I am so thankful that this process…has so effectively increased the number of literature evangelists, their total sales, as well as their average income while reducing the total dependence on each conference and union's tithe."

But the president's optimism had a hollow ring to those of us who knew even a little about the dire financial situation at FER. I was mystified by the president's wholesale misrepresentation of what I knew to be the facts. Why would he hazard his reputation and good name by putting such wishful thinking in writing? I had been associated with the audit of FER for the year ending December 31, 1993, and even then we questioned whether or not the company could continue to function financially for more than one year. We saw that the revenues seemed supported largely by receivables from the anticipated future sale of Bible videos — or, as one of my old Filipino friends used to call them, "deceivables."

The 1994 audit of FER was completed after my departure, but it was clear by then that its financial condition had dramatically worsened. But my successor in auditing apparently turned a blind eye to the situation, and he allowed an unsupported $2 million note receivable for "future video income" to be listed on the balance sheet. FER's debt level had by then surpassed a staggering $4 million.

In March 1996, the month the promised animated "Bible stories" had been set to launch across North America, Otis editorialized in the *Columbia Union Visitor*, under the heading "Risk for God," that "the Church must be willing to try new things. When we are willing to take calculated, prayed-over risks, the Lord enables us to accomplish things that would otherwise seem impossible!"

In a not-so-subtle way, Otis was suggesting that those who challenged his venture were in league with the devil, and that the evil one wanted the Church to "take timid steps [rather] than to risk for God." Then Otis drew from his deep study of Ellen White's writings and pointed out "that people with financial resources not of our faith would come forward to help spread the Gospel 'like the leaves of autumn.'"

This bombshell closed with the incredible news that "a total of $18 million of non-Adventist money had been dedicated to developing and marketing this series of fifteen videos."

Perhaps no one person can adequately comprehend the principal reason for the downfall of the ill-conceived FER organization. Clearly one reputedly "ruthless" man was minding the store, while others stood by, concerned but silent. But some voices spoke out, such as Bruce Wickwire's, a respected, retired world publishing leader, who wrote repeated letters of caution. Certainly part of the problem was Otis's cherished dream of becoming known as the father of an animated video series of "Bible stories."

Furthermore, the scheme to parlay $363,000 of illegally borrowed money into a fund of millions was clearly doomed. Within a few months of Folkenberg's glowing report, FER was dead in the water.

In November 1996 the FER Study Taskforce was established to investigate the events leading to FER's failure. Martin told the Taskforce that "FER leadership was certain that this project would succeed, and we felt it was best to give them the opportunity [money] to try."

The Taskforce presented its report to the Columbia Union Executive Committee on January 10, 1997, where it was clearly stated that Martin, Lee, and Russell had all been well aware that they were circumventing the Columbia Union Executive Committee in releasing the $363,000.

How could they be oblivious to the extreme risk they were taking in advancing union funds for such a project? Still, in spite of the Taskforce's critical report, the Executive Committee accepted Martin and Lee's apologies, and life went on.

But two conferences in the union did not take so kindly to the reports. The Potomac Conference voted to ask Martin and Lee to submit their resignations, and the Ohio Conference Executive Committee voted to ask the Union Executive Committee to call a special constituency meeting to explore FER issues and determine if Martin had the credibility to continue as president. So the Columbia Union Executive Committee met on January 30, 1997 to consider the requests, and McClure, then president of the North American Division, presided (supposedly to insure impartiality). The committee predictably denied the Ohio Conference's request for a special constituency meeting and reaffirmed Ralph Martin's position as president, with an added commitment to support his leadership!

Laymen were astounded! Given Martin's lack of judgment in essentially stealing funds from the Church to loan to FER, what redeeming characteristics allowed him to hold onto his job, uncensured? What company, large or small, would tolerate such mismanagement? But the Church, once again, seemed incapable of establishing executive discipline. Not only was Martin allowed to retire in good graces, after 41 years of denominational service; he was succeeded as president by his cohort, Harold Lee!

Much could have been salvaged, perhaps, had my successor in auditing frankly questioned the paltry, paper profits of $735 in 1994 and $38,241 in 1995. I know these auditors were qualified—they did not fail through incompetence. But as it turns out, FER actually lost $1.5 million during those two years and papered over the loss with a $2.4 million note receivable for "anticipated sales of the 'Bible Story' video."

Why the auditors became involved in the cover-up surpasses my ability to credibly speculate. I can only conjecture that they were intimidated by what had happened to me—they feared their jobs were at stake if they spoke up, so they stood silently by, as they had a year before when I was terminated. So nine months later, it was belatedly discovered that FER had actually lost yet another $1.29 million, and at that point the underpinnings gave way and the venture collapsed. The Columbia Union's loss was estimated at between $1.3 and $1.8 million, and it was recommended that the losses be amortized over the next five years. With the fall of FER, the Church's publishing ministry in the three affected unions was effectively consigned to languishing decline, except among select ethnic minorities.

Chapter 10:
Severing the Bond

Early in his administration, Robert Folkenberg chose Vice President Bob Kloosterhuis to serve as liaison between his office and the Auditing Service. Kloosterhuis, who had a better business orientation than most presidential personnel, quickly became a loyal advocate and supporter of the auditing program—a source of frustration for Folkenberg, who wanted me moved out of the picture.

But rather than choosing Kloosterhuis as the hatchet person to effect my termination, Folkenberg apparently believed the smooth, persuasive, often crafty Mittleider stood a better chance of finding a way to remove me from office, before the next General Conference Session. I once had considered Mittleider a friend; but I knew that first and foremost he was a politician.

During the summer of 1994, Folkenberg's boyhood friend Ben Maxson, whom he had called from the Upper Columbia Conference to promote GC stewardship, returned from the Northwest with a report that an emotionally disturbed woman in Oregon was willing to testify that many years before I had molested her. The news seemed to galvanize

Folkenberg and Mittleider. The young woman, whom Charlotte and I had known and whom Charlotte had befriended and counseled in the Far East, had been undergoing psychological therapy in Ohio, where thoughts and memories she had never consciously experienced or mentioned before were said to have surfaced.

Walter Carson, a GC attorney and member of the General Counsel staff, was sent to Ohio to meet with my accuser, Elizabeth "Beth" Heisler Olson Adels. Folkenberg apparently sensed that in Adventism there is no better way to administer a coup de grace to a troublesome presence than to brand him a sexual sinner.

Beth, who was now about 33, had failed once in marriage and was seemingly having difficulties in her second marriage. She apparently had had a number of extramarital affairs, and while attending the Oregon Camp Meeting, her husband had indeed surprised her with another man—an incident she refers to in her testimony against me as "being raped," though Camp Meeting personnel of that era recall no reports of a rapist, and Clackamas County authorities have no record of such a crime occurring on the heavily secured Campgrounds.

Suffice it to say, Beth's second marriage was in trouble, and she had journeyed to a psychological counseling center operated by Adventists in Ohio, where she had now "recalled" certain events that she believed had set her down the wrong pathway. Among these memories was her recollection that she had had an ongoing illicit affair with me. Beth was apparently earnest in her efforts to salvage her second marriage, and being able to report to her husband that she had had an affair with me, a family friend and father figure, seemingly helped her explain to herself, to her psychologist, and to her husband why she may have developed problems.

Attorney Carson worked with Beth and prepared a lengthy, sordid account and had it notarized as an affidavit, to give it every appearance of legitimacy. He brought the document back to the General Conference, and on the first day of the 1994 Annual Council, in early October, I was summoned to Carson's office, where he and Mittleider told me to read the document.

My family was well acquainted with the accuser, Beth, who at age 15 had come to live temporarily in our home in Singapore during the 1974-75 school year. Her parents were missionaries in Penang, Malaysia, and had become concerned because Beth was having difficulties relating to authority figures in her life, and had become suicidal. So we had agreed to allow Beth to stay in our home, with Cheryl, our own daughter, who was in the same grade. During those months, Charlotte spent many hours with Beth, trying to help her better relate to life.

Now, her affidavit brought three specific charges: That I had given her inappropriate backrubs when she was sharing our daughter's bedroom in Singapore; that I had met with her again and groped her, in Singapore, when I had returned for auditing work; and that 12 years before, she and I had met in a Tennessee motel room for a tryst. She could not recall the name of the motel, but claimed that she was sure that she and I had engaged in a sexual encounter.

Carson and Mittleider eagerly awaited my reaction. I was stunned and quickly assured them that I was totally innocent of the charges. The account was so muddled and wrong. Much of the wording was couched in psychological jargon clearly suggested by some form of "memory therapy" in vogue at the time.

Only eternity will reveal if Carson and Mittleider truly believed Beth's story, but at the time it seemed unimaginable. I recognized immediately, of course, how difficult it would be to conclusively prove my innocence, decades after the alleged events supposedly had taken place. But Mittleider clearly sought to rattle my composure further by telling me that he had defrocked many ministers for sexual improprieties, including the late Laverne Tucker, former Your Quiet Hour speaker. If I chose to "fight the charges" it would "get nasty," he threatened.

I asked for time to discuss the accusations with my wife, and I met with Charlotte, who was working that day nearby in the GC complex. We prayed together, then went back to meet with my prosecutors. Charlotte told them that logistically it would have been impossible for me to have met with Beth as she charged, but Mittleider unbelievably replied that God had given him special insights in dealing with sex offenders, and that if she defended me, that this was further evidence in his eyes that I was guilty! What manipulative logic! What Satanic reasoning! During my one and only visit to Tennessee since returning to the States from mission service, Charlotte had been with me as we visited several friends, including Beth and her family. There had been absolutely no opportunity whatever for me to have met privately with Beth — and Charlotte told him so.

But the two men would listen to none of it and pursued me relentlessly in the hallways, demanding that I resign. I explained that if Folkenberg had wanted me to resign, all he would have had to do was ask — then I would have tendered my resignation without hesitation. But now that I was being charged with evil I had not committed, to resign would appear to be an admission of guilt—and this I would not do.

At a later meeting, I told them that their treatment was becoming very adversarial, and that perhaps I should hire my own legal counsel. Carson concurred that I should, but I had never before been involved in litigation, and I found that locating the right lawyer was no easy task.

When I finally hired an attorney, he told the GC men that all communication between the organization and me would henceforth be handled through his office. This incensed my prosecutors all the more. Carson sent a certified letter, advising me that a hearing was planned, but that my attorney, Richard Swick, a committed Christian with an office in Washington, D.C., was not invited. I would be allowed only one person with me in the room, for support, or someone who would give testimony on my behalf—one or the other. My first impression was to refuse to dignify such an event with my presence. But Swick encouraged me to attend, though I was persuaded this was nothing but a lynching—and in retrospect, it was.

Every possible arrangement had been made to make me look as guilty as possible, and in that meeting and in the course of weeks to come, the stage was set, and after at least seven hours of discussion, my termination squeaked through with a less than 70 percent vote (a 2/3rds vote was required).

Then came a terse and threatening letter from Ruth Parish, director of the GC Office of Human Resources, advising me that a "settlement" of approximately $12,000 awaited me if I would sign a document, promising not to press charges or litigation against those who had driven me out of office. I disregarded the letter, but was amazed that not one GC employee would now speak with me or offer me help. The shunning was absolute!

I began working my way through the experience, and though I had an attorney, not once did it occur to me to bring any sort of legal action. I had no desire to sue my Church, the apple of my eye. Surely a hand of reconciliation would be offered.

So I asked for the arbitration of a neutral grievance committee, provided for by denominational policy, and sent the request to Matthew Bediako, the GC vice president who had presided during the final termination vote. A swift letter of denial came, clearly not written by Bediako, who hails from Ghana, West Africa, and has a distinctive style of writing. I phoned and asked him to confirm that he had indeed written the letter, and he admitted that he had signed a letter composed for him by Mittleider. But the message remained the same—I would be granted no hearing before a grievance committee. Clearly my detractors believed that I had come to the end of my reach.

But I recommitted myself to God's leading and made yet another offer of conciliation—I truly wished to avoid engaging in a protracted legal conflict, with its inherent public spectacle. Eventually I even offered to drop the matter, in lieu of the severance pay, if the GC would continue my salary an additional five months to provide me a total of 35 years of service credit—which would allow me to retire at age 62. This request, too, was summarily rejected.

With my sole legal counselor, we reviewed my legal options, and early in 1995, Swick sent a letter to the General Conference officers, outlining the legal brief we were prepared to file. He expressed my concern that defending the Church in court would be expensive, and that negative publicity might well develop. He proposed what we believed was a just and fair settlement—a settlement that we estimated would cost the Church less than a tenth of what a legal battle would entail.

But rather than settling, the GC immediately engaged three large legal firms in the Washington area, including the prestigious firm of Williams and Connally, to quash my initiatives. These lawyers urged Swick to go ahead and file our "frivolous" action, so on February 4, 1995, we followed their counsel and filed a straightforward suit in the District Court for Montgomery County, Maryland, home county of the GC.

We realized that the legal barriers in trying to bring a suit against a religious body were daunting, and that the GC would probably strategize to have the case dismissed on First Amendment grounds (which in the United States does not permit the entanglement of church and state business). So we filed a simple employment suit, claiming damages on three key issues: (1) wrongful discharge; (2) breach of contract; and (3) defamation. We asked only for a monetary settlement—we felt it would be legal suicide to ask for the return of my job and denominational credentials.

Then began the long waiting game with our nation's cumbersome legal system. Finally, the General Conference responded to our action, which we had brought against Robert Folkenberg, Alfred McClure, K. G. Mittleider, Walter Carson, and, of course, Elizabeth "Beth" Heisler Olson Adels, who had signed the affidavit of accusations against me. The GC had been careful not to provide us with any information on how they had persuaded Beth to testify as she did, how much money they may have given her, or why they had fired me just shy of my 35-year service anniversary, which effectively denied me significant pension benefits.

Charlotte and I feared that our meager personal resources would be inadequate to meet Goliath in this legal battle, but we were able to keep the case in court for seven years — during a time when the GC, by its own chosen course of action, managed to spend what we estimate to be in excess of $6 million to defend itself.

Some conservative Church members have criticized me for bringing this lawsuit, since the Bible speaks against "suing your brother." I seriously doubt that my suit against the Church corporation can in any sense be construed as legal action against a "brother," yet I regret the high-level decisions by the Church to spend so much tithe money in court. The denomination in this case impressed me more with its money, than its brains.

I had reviewed the biblical admonitions about lawsuits, written principally by the Apostle Paul. And in Chapter 40 of *Acts of the Apostles*, written by Ellen G. White, she says that Paul knew that he would not receive justice from the Jewish Sanhedrin, so he appealed his case to Caesar, for he too had been falsely accused by those who wished to end his career.

I saw clearly that our appeal through secular courts directly paralleled Paul's situation. Like Paul, I had been denied a just and unbiased hearing by my Church. I also considered that for years, the GC had been bringing baseless legal actions against individuals and institutions, never feeling the least bit constrained by biblical counsel. How, then, could I be faulted for seeking redress in court? Even as my action was before the courts, the GC sued an individual Church member for using the name

"Seventh-day Adventist" in reference to his Sabbath-keeping congregation in Florida, and such "trademark" actions continue to this day. The Church clearly feels that suing others is biblically permissible, provided the cause is just and no other recourse is available.

At last the time came for pre-trial discovery. The highly paid GC-contracted attorneys convinced my counsel that I should go first, and I underwent four days of bantering and harassment by the panel of opposing lawyers—two from each of the three law firms, plus Carson and Mittleider from the GC. Apparently they hoped to press me to confess to some wrongdoing, and that failing, simply discourage me from continuing to demand legal justice. They employed personal insults and gestures in the courtroom, but their efforts failed to rile us.

So they targeted my family. Charlotte performed impressively in the two-day session she faced. Then the attorneys interrogated my children—the meanest part of the Church's strategy. Their undisputed purpose was to try to create division within our family, and to this day our children harbor great mistrust of what they see as a basely corrupt and evil-spirited religious system. During these 10 days of recorded testimony, alone, the GC spent some $400,000 in legal expenses. Now, we figured, it was our turn to ask some questions.

But, incredibly, the GC immediately filed a motion asking that the process be stalled, nor was it now willing to submit any documentary evidence to us. It based its appeal on the premise that to give us the right to a jury trial would cause the secular court to "become entangled" (an expression used repeatedly) with Church business. This, of course, was exactly what we wanted the courts to do, and doing so would have saved the Church millions of dollars. But the GC seemed determined to keep the matter out of court entirely, stating and restating its position that it was exempt from any secular review of that which was done in an ecclesiastical setting. In effect, it was arguing that even if it committed murder in the course of its churchly business, it could remain exempt from prosecution by claiming its First Amendment rights!

The Church's attorneys would repeatedly argue and reargue this point for six years straight, and I would learn without a shadow of doubt that money can and does matter in legal decisions. As it turned out, during the entire span of years, we obtained not a single document, nor did anyone at the GC submit to a single deposition. At one point, the General Conference appeared to be running scared, when the Maryland State Supreme Court remanded the case back to the lower court, rather than assent to its request to have the case summarily dismissed, on First Amendment grounds. Above all else, the GC wanted to keep this whole matter quiet, out of the public eye and the scrutiny of a trial.

So GC lawyers changed tactics and informed the District Court judge, James Chapin, that as internal auditor I served in the capacity of a "highly elected official" of the Church. At this point, the intimidating retinue of attorneys seemed to break the resolve of the frail Chapin, and he agreed to conduct a "trial within a trial" on the issue of whether or not ecclesiastical issues overrode civil law, in my case.

My attorney strenuously objected and told the judge that the litigation was a matter of civil law and should proceed to a jury trial. But he was overruled, and in September 2001 we met in the Rockville, Maryland, chambers of the court for three days.

To this hearing the GC brought forward a number of Church employees. Folkenberg was conspicuously absent, but Neal Wilson was introduced as the former "pope" of the Church, with his "cardinals" represented by former secretary Ralph Thompson, the GC treasurer, Robert Rawson, and the auditor who had replaced me, Eric Korff.

During this hearing the GC attempted to demonstrate that the auditor was not really "independent," but was an elected official of the Church. We were stunned as they alleged that it was required that the chief auditor be ordained as a gospel minister! This was absolutely false — I was the first chief auditor in Church history to be ordained, and Korff was only the second! We had both been ordained while serving the Church in other capacities, before being employed as auditors. My ordination was entirely independent of my election as chief auditor. Indeed, my predecessor, Ralph Davidson, served with dignity as the chief auditor for a number of years, without the benefit of ordination. And as of this writing, the current chief auditor (who has replaced Korff) is not an ordained minister. The Church clearly was willing to risk a conviction of perjury to avoid having to answer my suit in court.

Under strong pressure from the six attorneys representing the GC, the elderly judge in late September 2001 ruled that the GC and its officers were indeed immune from litigation, under First Amendment privilege, and declared that my termination was an "ecclesiastical matter." He died of natural causes a few weeks later.

I will never know in this life what factors influenced the judge to draw a conclusion in law that took away my right to trial by jury. My attorney had told me of a meeting to which I was not invited in the private chambers of Judge Chapin. There, grossly outnumbered by the defendant's attorneys, Swick had pled in vain for the case to move forward to trial.

Immediately the ruling was trumpeted far and wide, through the official Church media, as a "victory." It may have been a victory for the Church to be able to hide its wrongful conduct on First Amendment grounds, but true "winning" would have involved convincing a jury that the Church had acted fairly in my termination. My family and our descendants will never be able to answer the question: "If, as claimed, there was evidence to convict me of sexual impropriety, why did the Church work so diligently, and at such expense, to avoid going to trial?" What was really behind the maneuvering?

Furthermore, Church members will never receive a full accounting of the millions of dollars, tithe and non-tithe, spent so the Church would not have to defend itself in court.

Chapter 11:
The Theology of Tithe

While spending millions of dollars to keep my case from going to trial (one of many of its ongoing litigations at the time), the Church continued making its persistent appeals for members to "sacrifice" to prepare for the Lord's Second Coming.

While employed by the Church, I had obediently practiced and promoted tithing, exactly as prescribed by the Church. I had referred to unpaid tithes as "robbing God," in the words of Malachi 3. I had used Jesus' comment that "this [tithing] you should have done and not to have left the other undone." Blessings did indeed seem to follow those who returned their tithes, and my parents had always testified to the peace of mind it brought them. Still, the position taken by the Church—making tithing almost an 11th commandment—seemed to call for a second look. Furthermore, applying the word "storehouse" to local conference offices takes some exegetical doing. Adventists have formed many independent ministries outside the denominational umbrella, and these participate in Gospel proclamation. They are divided into two groups—those recognized by the General Conference (such as Amazing Facts and The Quiet

Hour) and those out of favor with the denomination (such as Hartland Institute, Hope International, and Steps to Life). Both groups evangelize and teach the Church's fundamental doctrines, with the one distinction that the approved institutions claim to forward all tithe monies on to local conferences, while those out of favor openly use tithe funds in their own ministries.

Now, tithe sent to the "approved" ministries are by no means always used as the donor designates them. During my years as director of Auditing Service, I was an invitee to regular meetings of the Church's treasurers—presumably as a resource person on matters relating to accounting practices. One day I was summoned to the conference room on the main floor of the new GC complex to meet with the GC treasury group. Treasurer Don Gilbert called the meeting to order with prayer, and then presented the dilemma at hand. A cashier's check for $5,000 in U.S. currency had arrived some days before, from the Canadian province of Alberta. An accompanying letter stated that the donors, who identified the funds as "tithe," wished to have the dollars forwarded to assist family members in Zaire in mission work. The "missionary family in Africa" at that time turned out to be that of Bob Lemon, who would later become GC treasurer, himself.

The associate GC treasurer assigned to receipt and acknowledge such donations had dutifully returned the check with a polite letter, advising the would-be donors that Church policy prohibited accepting tithe funds for out-of-conference use. He advised the tithe-payer that the money should properly be contributed through the Alberta Conference.

Now came the frustrating part: the check had been re-contributed, with an accompanying letter that read, "You do not understand. This is our tithe and we want it to go to help our missionary family, the Lemons, in Zaire. You ask us to pay this to the Alberta Conference. Just for your information, we are not Seventh-day Adventists and members of your church; we are Baptists."

What to do? We discussed the matter with something less than fully professional acumen, recognizing that to send the money back would probably mean that it would be donated to some Baptist coffer.

Finally, with a degree of eloquence, one of the treasurers said, "This should not be a problem for us. If the money comes from Baptists, it's not really 'tithe' anyway." Decision made! The funds were receipted through the GC accounts and forwarded for missionary work in Africa.

After college I had worked in the Iowa Conference treasury, where one of my titles was that of "associate auditor." One of my first assignments was to keep an up-to-date log sheet of the local church treasurers' reports. The log listed every Church employee, pastor, teacher, or credentialed colporteur in the conference, and beside each name I faithfully noted each person's tithe contributions. Based on my high-level snooping, several reprimands went out and in one case an employee was transferred out of the conference for delinquencies in tithing.

Adventist theology, especially in financial matters, seems to be based on three sources: (1) the Bible, (2) the writings of Ellen White, and (3) voted Church policies. Most would agree that Scriptural commands hold precedence, with Ellen White's inspired counsels serving as corollaries. But Church policies change with whims of the times, and their authority does not match those of the Bible or of Ellen White.

Yet, Church administrators seem to treat all three as equally binding. During my legal battle with the GC, attorneys repeatedly told the court that the GC is "the highest authority of God on earth" — thereby appropriating for the Church one of the papacy's central claims.

Tithe is supposedly used only to compensate those engaged in Gospel ministry and evangelistic outreach, but the Church also allows it to be used to pay for janitorial services of the various conference offices and to subsidize church school teachers' salaries. And millions in unaccounted-for tithe dollars are invested in prolonged and unproductive lawsuits.

The New Testament gives little counsel on tithe paying, and Church policy has come to dictate how tithe funds are to be used. In the New Testament, followers of Jesus are encouraged to "give up all" to follow Him (Matthew 19:21), and to have "all things in common" (Acts 2:44). There is no mention of segregated giving in Scripture. I can only conclude that tithing, in the manner of modern Adventism, is primarily a fund-raising vehicle — with a provision attached that causes Church members to feel a moral obligation to give 10 percent of their increase to this segregated fund. Furthermore, we find nowhere in Scripture any specific definition of "the storehouse." Yet Church policy determines as a matter of faith that the storehouse is indeed the conference office. If Desmond Ford got into ecclesiastical hot water for questioning the Church's position on the Investigative Judgment, one can imagine the furor caused if someone were to stand in the pulpit and challenge the Church's lack of biblical authority on tithing. In fact, a few years ago it happened in Portland, Oregon and the then-prominent pastor in question was immediately fired.

But as an experienced auditor, I can say without equivocation that the abuses in the use of tithe are even more egregious than abuses in its collection. More disconcerting than any deception created in promoting the tithing concept is the typical lack of transparency in properly reporting how the tithe is actually used.

How does it happen that the expenditure of millions in tithe dollars for prolonged litigation is approved? Actually, such approval comes from a very tight circle of administrators. Appropriate committees, such as the General Conference Executive Committee, are never consulted and there is no recorded committee action authorizing massive outlays for litigation. Furthermore, nothing about these vast expenditures in tithe dollars is ever reported in denomination-controlled publications. Decisions of this nature are typically made by only two or three officers, in counsel with highly compensated GC-employed attorneys. They then engage prestigious law firms who, with carte blanche, charge unimaginably large sums. How can this kind of behavior be justified in a Church that forbids its own members from taking one another to court?

Rather than demanding accountability, however, many members seem to prefer knowing nothing about these inconsistencies—and the Church public relations arm accommodates them in every way. I experienced this kind of "brainwashing" as a child, growing up Adventist. If the Church said it was true, I was to accept it! We were told to give our offerings, regardless of how the money was handled. I saw this again during the Davenport loan debacle, when members pled with the *Adventist Review* not to write "negative" articles. Again, when Folkenberg's financial improprieties were made known, the Church press presented an "all's well" spin.

But let's look again at the Church's policy on tithe—an area where as an auditor I have a great deal of experience. Policy specifically prohibits use of tithe for teachers' salaries and capital expenditures. But during the past 25 years, by implementing fund accounting principles, it was disclosed that the Church has been circumventing policy. For example, most funds used for everyday overseas mission work come from tithe, but are not restricted to direct support of the ministry. It poses an embarrassing conundrum, and the policy either needs to be changed or accounting transactions altered. Typically, these matters are ignored as long as possible. But eventually, perhaps, committees will be set up to study the situation and make recommendations.

Due at least in part to the theology of tithe, Adventists are recognized as generous givers. But, unlike members of other denominations, the percentage of funds Adventist congregations send on to conferences and unions is so high (more than 70 percent) that it is often difficult for them to build and maintain their local church buildings, let alone promote high-profile ministry in the community.

But happy signs now lead me to believe that blind acceptance of such policies is on the wane. Elderly Church members rarely question the current tithing apportionments, but the younger and more highly educated are looking for constructive ways to make their contributions go further. More and more Church members are giving to support specific projects, rather than giving to funds where donations are arbitrarily used for salaries and other overhead costs.

Chapter 12:
The Spiritless Gift of Gossip

A shocking fallout from the way the Church treated Charlotte and me emerged later as character cannibalism, remarkably doled out by a membership that claims to be largely vegetarian.

After my termination, former colleagues and friends started dashing through the supermarket or ducking into their cars to avoid crossing our paths. At the time, we had no idea what was actually being said about us. For all we knew, high tech methods were spreading the smear campaign to the ends of the earth, and as it turned out, the General Conference had even participated in the creation of articles published about us in large American newspapers, including the *Washington Times* and the *Los Angeles Times*.

As this book goes to press, 14 years later, we can sympathize with the Scriptural lepers who ran about shouting "unclean." I remember so well visiting Adventist churches in various parts of the United States, where we would have otherwise been unknown, and signing the guest registers with my mother's maiden name, Taylor. By then everyone recognized the name "David Dennis," and had I given my real name, we would have become a gaping-stock.

Some have marveled that we did not simply drop our Adventist membership. But why should we, when we subscribe in principle to its beliefs? What I do find truly amazing is that no one involved in the campaign to end my career has yet stepped forward to seek my forgiveness, or offered so much as to shake my hand. I have forgiven them, but there has been no reconciliation—not even one attempt.

Choirmaster among the gossipers was Ken Mittleider, who spread lies around the globe, like the leaves of autumn. In one address to his fellow officers in a GC Administrative Committee (ADCOM) meeting, early in 1995, he is said to have alleged that eight more women had come forward to accuse me of sexual impropriety. Barbara Middag, his confidant and office co-worker, also repeated reports of my "misconduct"—all of which she says she verified personally.

Even some of my old friends succumbed to the allure of the campaign against Charlotte (she was reviled as "a conniver, a dupe, a codependent") and me. Larry Colburn and his wife, Carole, joined the litany, though we had once considered them among our best friends. At one stage, I would have pointed to Larry as my character reference of choice, for we served together as missionary neighbors in Jakarta and had been close associates for nearly 40 years.

Only eternity will reveal the extent of the slander they spread. Larry served for several years as personal assistant to Robert Folkenberg, and may have become involved in some of Folkenberg's investments—it wouldn't surprise me. After Folkenberg left office, I wrote to Folkenberg's successor, Jan S. Paulsen, in October 2001, inviting Christian closure to the GC's attacks against me. Colburn responded, on November 12, 2001, asking me, in turn, to "leave this difficult chapter behind."

I was pleased, and accepted at face value Colburn's urging that we all move on. But what was my surprise, when I found that a Church member in Hemet, California, had written to Paulsen on August 27, 2002, asking for a resolution of my case. Forthwith, Colburn responded to the Church member on September 12, 2002, stating that "the Church" had "adequate evidence" to convict me! This message was then widely circulated over the Internet, opening a whole new round of questions, allegations, and speculations.

Feeling betrayed, I wrote him again on October 8, 2002, admonishing him for breaking faith with his earlier letter. He replied by letter on October 16 with pithy blather about the need for forgiveness. Yet neither Colburn nor his superiors ever came to me and asked me to forgive them for any of their behavior. Apparently Church officials at some level cease making mistakes—to admit to the possibility would be to deny the Church's institutional infallibility! How faithfully the Church has come to duplicate that poker-faced, uncompromising intransigence it so abhors in the papacy!

Here the name of Thomas E. Wetmore bears mentioning, a Church-employed attorney chosen by GC chief counsel Robert Nixon to help direct an after-the-fact propaganda war against me. Here's a sample of Wetmore's inflammatory writing, in an e-mail letter dated November 30, 2001:

"Frankly nobody from this house [GC] wants to help [Mr. Dennis] keep his diatribe alive by responding to [him] in anyway (stet). Certainly from my standpoint, as counsel for the Church, neither I nor anyone within earshot of my counsel will enter into dialog with [him]....about any of his allegations, claims, [or his] agenda...We have just successfully concluded a long legal battle with him over his spurious claims of defamation and have no interest in giving him a new opportunity to launch a similar attack against the Church."

Then, as a follow-up to my friend's observations, Wetmore reprised on December 5 with these diplomatic thoughts:

"[Inviting Mr. Dennis to] dialog with anyone in Church leadership is very much like [asking] Osama bin Ladin to address the UN on topics of world peace, US government reform and global evangelical objectives and strategies for Christianity....Whatever [Mr. Dennis] has to say on ANY topic will be viewed with the same degree of suspicion and skepticism as Osama bin Ladin....I am not overstating the matter in the slightest....Do you really expect anyone, except the lunatic fringe, to take [his] ideas seriously?"

Those who query Wetmore about the GC's appeals to have the case dismissed because of First Amendment privilege are told that the GC possesses "overwhelming evidence" against me. Yet he fails to explain why the GC is unwilling to allow this evidence to be examined in a trial before a jury.

Another who has weighed in to judge and convict me in the court of Adventist public opinion is John Lorentz, ex-pastor of the Hendersonville, N.C. church. Lorentz stood before his congregation one Sabbath morning in early Spring 1995 and, calling me by name publicly, told the congregants that I had "20 illicit girlfriends." What amazes me even more is how readily Church parishioners seemed to accept these wild statements.

For some time Pastor Lorentz had been making frequent mission trips to Cuba, as a long-time associate of Folkenberg in Inter-America, and his Church members appreciated his evangelizing efforts on behalf of that renegade Caribbean island. But what no one knew at the time is that, in confirmation of Romans 2:1, the beloved pastor, himself, had a mistress in Cuba—and when this became known, his international proselytizing efforts came to an abrupt end!

The name of Phillip Follett also deserves mention, here, whose hatred toward me boiled over on more than one occasion. He had written me a letter a couple of years before my unceremonious departure from the GC, while he was still president of the Atlantic Union Conference, and I reviewed it during my final legal appeal. In it he expressed his discomfort with statements I had made in his hearing, and with which he disagreed—remarks in which I had simply advocated the need for Church leaders to be candid and open in the presentation of financial reports.

By 1994 Follett had become a GC vice president and was apparently assigned to visit each GC department to share information about my termination and to make sure I was publicly maligned and my reputation irredeemably shredded among my colleagues. His open meetings with the various departments and services, in our opinion, sowed the seeds for the gossip that festers to this day.

Yet another name worthy of mention is Eric Korff's, who was chosen to succeed me as head of Auditing Service. It had been said that for some time Korff had been laying the political groundwork to take over my job, though certainly it had never occurred to me that he did any such thing. He was simply my friend, and it was I, after all, who had rescued him from an upheaval in South Africa and had advocated his appointment as one of my GC associates. Unfortunately, I have concluded that his gift of opportunism surpasses even his accounting skills.

Korff was close with my chief prosecutor, Mittleider, with whom he had worked in Africa — and perhaps this had something to do with his appointment to my vacated job. The fact that he was an ordained minister may also have contributed to his election — as it strengthened the specious argument that only ordained ministers can serve as head auditors. No such provision has ever existed in policy, but it does seem opportune that Korff was the only one of 60 Church-employed auditors in North America who was ordained at the time. And to stir the pot a bit more, does this mean that a female CPA of skill and character was ineligible for the position of head auditor, since the Church refuses to recognize women through ordination?

Korff also obliged the brethren by setting up a meeting of associates and inviting Mittleider and Carson to spend two full days bringing the troops up to speed on the terrible things I had supposedly done — this being more or less the sole purpose of the meeting. He then instructed the entire auditing staff not to communicate with me in any way (and most have carefully complied). An office secretary who had kindly been mailing me little newssheets that listed auditing activities was told in no uncertain terms to stop sending me anything.

Roland A. Hegstad was for years my neighbor on Sondra Court in Silver Spring, Maryland, and a promoter of religious liberty for the General Conference. It seems ironic that one who touted "freedom of conscience," apparently came to support the view that I should be denied access to a fair jury trial. Hegstad in fact served as an advisor on how to persuade the judge to immunize the GC from legal review. I realize that Hegstad for at least a few moments must have been torn between his loyalty to the Church and his instinctive stand for the rights of the individual. Perhaps in younger years he would have stood resolutely for my right to challenge my accusers in a trial, fair and square. How sad that in the twilight of his career he chose to prefer the organization over the individual.

What bothers me most about his attitude was that when my son, Sam, stopped by Hegstad's home to visit our longtime friend. Hegstad told Sam that he too was the son of an adulterer and could sympathize with Sam's pain. Sam immediately left Hegstad's home in stunned disbelief to think that his "friend" had betrayed him in believing the lies about his father.

Was Hegstad truly convinced of my guilt and concerned for my son, or was he testing to see if wedges could be driven into the solidarity the Dennis family has held throughout this ordeal? All I know is that Hegstad not once has discussed the matter with me, though I have invited him to talk things over. He has always declined my overtures.

God has granted me the peace to forgive all these men and women. I only wish this forgiveness could someday lead to reconciliation—but I'm not holding my breath. This does not appear to be something we do well, as Church leaders. While we oppose the teaching "once saved, always saved," we seem determined to follow the opposite and even more destructive doctrine, "once branded, always branded."

Ellen White speaks eloquently to this point in a May 14, 1895, article in the *Review and Herald*: "When an effort is made to ascertain the truth in regard to those who have been represented as in the wrong, their accusers are frequently unwilling to grant them the benefit of a doubt as to the reliability of the evil reports. They seem determined that their accusations shall stand just as they have stated them, and they treat the accused as guilty without giving them a chance to explain. But when accusers manifest so fierce a determination to make a brother or sister an offender, and cannot be made to see or feel that their own course has been wrong, it is evident that the transforming power of the enemy has been upon them, and that he has caused them to reflect his attributes."

I don't hate my accusers, or the gossipers, as I staunchly believe that "it is evident that the transforming power of the enemy" was them and that he "caused them to reflect his attributes."

Chapter 13:

Adventist Leadership and Sex

S ome years ago a prominent Washington politician was spotted late one night, cavorting drunkenly with his concubine in the Tidal Basin. It generated quite a stir in the tabloids and the capital's social columns, but the man soldiered on in his political career. Yet I know that if the same legislator had been found illicitly holding $15,000 in public funds, without proper accounting, he would have been forced from office.

Several years after the good senator was spotted frolicking in the reflecting pools, Charles Bradford, president of the North American Division observed that while the government often winks at sexual impropriety, it comes down hard on those who abuse their fiduciary trust. The Church, he remarked, does the opposite. If a minister of the Gospel is found with a girlfriend, in any setting, he will be judged severely. If, on the other hand, he is suspected of embezzling a few thousand dollars from Church coffers, he may simply be moved to another parish.

But things have changed since the 1970s. In today's world, while a Church employee tagged with sexual impropriety may appear to receive swift and certain punishment, in the long run the punishment may be nominal. In my case, the GC brethren knew that the GC Committee would not fire me outright (many shared the view that visionaries require supervision, etc.) so a claim of misconduct was required to get the job done.

Ordinarily, in today's world, the Church gives every benefit of the doubt to popular denominational employees accused of sexual misconduct. I knew this, and during the discovery phase in my legal case, my attorney documented incredible cases where Adventist ministers accused of moral failings were assisted in their defense against their accusers. In the following paragraphs, I wish to illustrate historically the stark contrast between what the Church normally does and what happened in my case.

The Apostle Paul, writing in Romans 2:1, asserts that anyone who judges another is "guilty of the same thing." The charges brought against me were more than routine maneuvers to remove an undesired employee from a powerful position. What the Church did was fundamentally evil and taints us all.

As I watched, with sadness, the frenzy of gossip, it seemed that these men possessed an unusually ripe and ready store of creative accusations. I had learned long ago, in Church finance, that normally those most eager to accuse others of financial impropriety are thieves themselves. I point this out because of the many months it took me to accept the possibility that my own accusers may have had first-hand experience in the very kinds of behavior of which I was accused. I pray, by the grace of God, that I'm wrong.

What I do know is that while my case was still in litigation, the General Conference appointed James Gilley, a man with a seriously compromised marital past, as an officer of the North American Church. Yet, to impress the judge, the lawyers arrayed against me stated that in the Adventist Church, once an individual is found to have committed adultery, he or she can no longer hold Church office or carry credentials. Yet, Gilley continued to occupy a high Church office and pastor an area church until he retired, with ministerial credentials. He is now president of Three Angels Broadcasting Network.

The misdeeds of many in Church employment are known only to God. Some, of course, we know, which is why the GC worked so extraordinarily hard to keep my case from going to discovery and trial. There was absolutely no way the Church could have successfully defended its decision to drum me out of Church employment, while it continued to concede broad moral latitude to employees who were popular with administration, and/or had strong support among key groups of Church members.

In court documents we found the amazing story of Mitch Henson, senior pastor of the Beltsville, Maryland, Adventist church. For years he had carried on a liaison with the church's Bible worker, Patty Wilkinson. Later she married a man named Bunker—who naturally disapproved of the continuing relationship between his new wife and her pastor. So he filed a lawsuit, but the Church defended Henson, on grounds that the affair with Mrs. Bunker amounted only to oral sex, a fact she did not dispute. How refreshing to find that a pastor is free to engage in oral sex with married members of his congregation, without breaking the Seventh Commandment! Nonetheless, Henson then was carted across the country to pastor in California.

Some high-profile cases were hushed up so effectively that we were unable to figure out what really had happened. But what these cases do demonstrate is that Church officials normally try to cover up sexual scandals. The senior pastor of the large church at Southwestern Adventist University was accused of adultery, but because it could not be proven absolutely, the matter was dropped and the pastor was transferred to California.

A former pastor of the Pacific Union College church was accused by many women of adultery. The Church provided funding to help him prove his innocence, but it appears that his subsidized efforts for vindication failed, and he ultimately resigned.

An editor of one of the denomination's major periodicals was doing graduate study at Loma Linda University, when he was caught in the act of adultery by local law enforcement officials. He continues today as the president of one of North America's Adventist colleges.

Perhaps the most flagrant case of cover-up in recent history is that of Henry Wright. Hank (as he is called by many) was union secretary, during the presidency of Columbia Union's Ronald Wisbey. Hank is a gifted speaker and performed his work well, and to no one's surprise, when the GC sought to fill the position of ministerial secretary vacated at the retirement of Floyd Bresee, Hank was chosen for the post.

But a few hours later, a bombshell exploded, when Wright's girlfriend of many years called to tell him that if he accepted this new position, she would blow the whistle on their affair. According to records we obtained from a close relative, the girlfriend had become pregnant with Hank's child.

We recognize that all have sinned and fallen short of God's glory, but the incredible part of the Henry Wright saga is that Wisbey advised him how to stage his repentance and behavior in such a way as to avoid dismissal from Church work. Though Wright admitted that the woman's account was true, he was not required to relinquish his credentials, nor did he suffer a break in his service record. For years now he has remained a highly respected minister in the Potomac Conference and a sought-after guest speaker. He has served on the faculty of Columbia Union College and for years was considered a role model for aspiring young ministers.

These cases, involving men who were popular with administrators, contrast darkly with the treatment accorded me, a loathed whistle-blower—and in the United States, it is absolutely illegal to discriminate against employees simply because they happen to go beyond the call of duty in exposing institutional error. In fact, that's what all good auditors are paid to do; we are like canaries in the mine shaft who try to catch fatal accounts before they permeate and affect everybody. I always took that responsibility to heart.

Clearly it was decided to use Beth's charge against me, first to try to induce me to resign under fire, and that failing, to argue for my termination to the GC Committee. In either case, they would be disposing of an employee who seemed too eager to do his job as a watchdog. The 1980s had seen millions of Church dollars squandered in the wake of incompetent decisions by Church leaders, and I had determined that the 1990s would be different! They certainly were—with the first-ever resignation of a sitting GC president, due to financial impropriety, and the first-ever summary termination of a chief auditor of the Church.

A primary reason the brethren were so anxious to fire me is found in the closing arguments presented to the late Judge Chapin, when Neal Wilson explained that the fundamental problem was that I "lacked people skills." This is often brethren-speak for men and women who are willing and able to speak out on matters of simple right and wrong. Many thinking Church members want more of this quality in leadership, and their thoughts are frequently echoed in the writings of Ellen White, where she says that the greatest want in the world is for men who will not be bought and sold on the auction block of expediency.

When Beth's document, written with Carson's assistance, was thrust before me that morning in October 1994, I immediately detected Folkenberg's handiwork. Knowing of his reputation for revenge, I felt that the best course of action was to confront the matter head-on and meet the Christian standard of "going to your brother."

So before the committees and panels could be mobilized to "catapult the propaganda," as a recent American president once admitted doing, I phoned Folkenberg's office and asked his office secretary, Annette Stephens, for an appointment with the boss. From her voice, however, I detected that Folkenberg did not favor such a meeting, and predictably she called back to say that I should instead take my concerns to Mittleider.

I'm intrigued, today, that in years after my firing, Folkenberg is quoted as wringing his hands in anguish when questioned about my case, and hypocritically pleading, "What more could I have done?" I'll answer that question. For one, he could have accepted my overture to discuss things, man to man, as Christians.

Swick was more than just any attorney — as a Christian, he felt that since the General Conference professed Christian values, that we would be facing fine, decent men, eager to work out a fair accommodation, in the spirit of Christ. He had not realized yet how deeply the underlying currents ran against me.

Little wonder, then, that Swick's earnest efforts to resolve the case were met with volumes of costly, obstructing paperwork. Each judge involved in our suit earnestly encouraged both sides to settle, but Church attorneys always demanded that I admit my guilt in writing as a precondition. For political purposes, the Church was determined to force me either to admit guilt — or face financial ruin. As a long-time missionary, I had comparatively few assets, and they knew it. They must have believed that time was on their side — that I would eventually capitulate and admit, at least in part, that Beth's recollections fit the facts.

But to have said that her allegations were true would have been to compound a lie. Beth may have believed she was telling the truth, but Charlotte and I knew otherwise. Truth is truth, and cannot be compromised.

Perhaps the greatest evidence that the defendants were not proceeding in good faith was their legal trickery in avoiding giving depositions and providing documentation during the discovery process. Swick and my family members answered extensive questioning, under oath, for days on end — at any point, had the Church possessed solid evidence contradicting what we said, we could have been prosecuted for perjury. But we were sure in our testimony, sure of the facts.

But immediately after extracting this testimony from us, the GC's defense attorneys placed an interlocutory action on the case and appealed to the Maryland Supreme Court for dismissal on the basis of the First Amendment's "entanglement" clause. My attorney's error in judgment to allow our family to go to deposition without getting any information at all from the GC defendants caused years of delay and ended with the legal immunization of Church officials.

In court it would have been quite simple for us to prove how unfair the GC had been in rushing to convict me on charges far less credible than those leveled against many others who still held Church credentials. We'd done our research, and the case would have been ruled overwhelmingly in our favor. This the GC knew.

At a September 2001 final hearing before the judge, (available in the District Court of Montgomery County Maryland public records, under case no. 132721, dated February 22, 1995), former General Conference officers Neal Wilson and Ralph Thompson pled that the Church should be exempted from the case because the Adventist Church structure was so similar to the Roman Catholic Church's!

Indeed, one of their many attorneys, Deborah Whelihan, gushingly pointed to Wilson and said he was "just like the pope and his cardinals." Late in 2001, Swick phoned to advise me that Judge Chapin had ruled that we could no longer sustain an action against leaders of the Church. This left only one defendant, Beth, who by then had adopted an openly gay lifestyle and was said to be on the verge of personal bankruptcy, having lost the house she had received in settlement at her second divorce. It was pointless to pursue the case. The GC, meanwhile, exalted in its success at keeping the case out of court. It was a vindictive position, but hardly vindicating.

Chapter 14:

The Fall of Folkenberg

At the 55th Session of the General Conference in 1990, the newly elected president, Robert Stanley Folkenberg, first showed his hostility toward me. Only 15 months before, I had addressed and circulated my open letter to Neal Wilson, and the Nominating Committee, chaired by Folkenberg prior to his election, had determined to deny Wilson a third complete term.

The Nominating Committee first chose George Brown to replace him. Brown had been president of the fast-growing Inter-American Division since 1980, and was elected on the first ballot by the 226 Nominating Committee members. But the 66-year-old Brown rejected the offer almost immediately. Eyes then began turning toward the Nominating Committee chairman himself, the 49-year-old Robert Folkenberg, Brown's long-time associate in Inter-America.

A swell of support swept the then-relatively unknown Folkenberg into office, and the vote by the full body of delegates came only minutes before the session adjourned on Friday evening, before the Sabbath.

After his election, Folkenberg and his wife, Anita, seemed uncharacteristically cool toward Charlotte and me, as we approached them to extend our congratulations. Anita was the daughter of our friends, Ken and Dottie Emmerson. Ken Emmerson had served with distinction as GC treasurer for more than 12 years, and Dottie had been my secretary. I had known Folkenberg's parents, Stan and Barbara, from the days when he served as treasurer of the Central European Division in Bern, Switzerland, in the 1960s. So Charlotte and I felt connected to the Folkenbergs.

Now, Folkenberg by virtue of his office had become the direct liaison between the Auditing Service and the General Conference Committee, so I had every reason to wish to establish excellent rapport with the new executive.

But Charlotte and I both felt Folkenberg's disdain, that first evening. He typically found it easy to smile, but for us there was no friendliness when we congratulated him. In me, I believe, Folkenberg saw a dangerous auditor who carried things too far, who meddled in areas where a loyal team player should not dare to tread. During his years in the Inter-America Division, as a union president in Guatemala and division field secretary in Miami, he had flaunted his independence and apparently resented the few observations auditors had made regarding his direct fund-raising in North America and his personal use of a donated Piper Aztec.

In retrospect, the irregularities of his financial dealings, if known at that time, would not only have totally shocked auditors, but Church administrators as well, some of whom had themselves become accustomed to living on the ragged edge. I marvel that apparently no one with knowledge of those financial dealings was troubled enough to speak up before Folkenberg's election. Many who had worked with him in Central America had questions, but in the ethos of the Advent Movement, who were they to question the credibility of God's anointed?

Knowing now what the astute Folkenberg must have known in 1990 of his vulnerability to blackmail, I wonder why he accepted the presidency at all. Only four months before, on March 20, 1990, he had tendered $53,000 to a California Superior Court to mitigate the prison sentence of his long-time friend and business colleague, James E. Moore. Moore had been convicted on eight counts of grand larceny and had been incarcerated in December 1989. Could thoughts of Moore's lock-up be far from Folkenberg's mind as he accepted the presidential nomination? Was he thinking of his friend Moore when he penned these words in his acceptance speech?: "I believe fervently that there is no challenge so deep, no difficulty so apparently unsolvable, that the Lord cannot provide the answer."

He apparently believed that the president of the world Church could not, and would not, be called to task for his financial mistakes.

Among the many virtues cited in Folkenberg was his creative vision. Ramón Maury, who had served as Inter-American Division treasurer since 1980, drew me aside during the discussion of Folkenberg's nomination as president and knowingly warned me, "Men of vision need supervision."

Others commented that Folkenberg had fabulous business instincts, though I never personally saw this trait in the man. Yes, he was a born salesman and innovator, and could raise fabulous sums of money. But his business acumen left a great deal to be desired, especially in ethical matters.

I believe Folkenberg set out to destroy my career as payback for my whistle-blowing on the matter of his wife's compensation through the Columbia Union Worthy Student Fund and others of my warnings that had affected some of his ventures. He apparently believed that he possessed the ability and capital to satisfy the growing restlessness of his friend, Moore. In my February 22, 1995, motion filed with the District Court of Montgomery County, I addressed many of Folkenberg's fiscal excesses. Had the Church at that time taken my warnings seriously, Folkenberg would not have been reelected in 1995 and much heartache could have been saved. But instead the General Conference officially labeled my claims "frivolous."

So nearly four more years of cover-up dragged on before Folkenberg's judgment hour came. The "handwriting on the wall" arrived in the form of a lawsuit that charged fraud against Folkenberg and other defendants, in the Sacramento County Superior Court, on August 21, 1998.

No one knows how much foreknowledge Folkenberg had, but like the Babylonians caught when the Medes burst under their walls, Folkenberg had been weighed in the balances and found wanting. Those named in the suit along with Folkenberg were the likes of Benjamin Kochenower, CPA, of North Carolina, who for years had prepared Folkenberg's income tax returns and served as a personal confidant; Terry Carson and his brother, Attorney Walter Carson, who had served as a personal attorney for Folkenberg's business ventures, while employed all the while in the GC Office of General Counsel. Terry Carson assisted his brother and Folkenberg in accumulating moonlighting income. Yet another defendant named was Duane McBride, on staff at Andrews University in Michigan and a pollster and researcher in Folkenberg's quest to revamp General Conference governance; Robert Dolan, a promoter and business associate in Folkenberg's real estate venture, known as Kanaka Valley Associates, was also cited.

Last, but not least, the Inter-American Division itself was named — that mission field where Folkenberg was employed when Moore and he began their pas de deux.

The legal action filed against him by Moore did not seem to surprise Folkenberg, and he apparently believed it could be resolved quietly. After all, Folkenberg had been doing everything in his power to assist Moore in his business plans and fund-raising. He had even used the influence of his office to write a letter of introduction for Moore to Archbishop Desmond Tutu, in South Africa.

Closer to home, Folkenberg had pressured the Adventist Disaster Relief Agency (ADRA) offices to join with Moore in a telecommunications venture. So the lawsuit seemed like a stab in Folkenberg's back, as Moore was trying to curry favor with the Roman Catholic Church.

Using typical legal jargon, the Church-engaged attorneys responded that the suit was "frivolous and without merit." But severe conflicts surrounded the case, not the least of which was Carson's personal involvement in the business venture itself. It bears repeating here that Folkenberg had selected Walter Carson as one of the two primary agents assigned to oust me from the General Conference. Now, to protect Carson from further public exposure on the Moore matter, Carson's superior, Robert Nixon, worked with Folkenberg and through the General Conference officers to obtain several hundreds of thousands of dollars from the Directors and Officers Liability insurance policy, purchased from Chubb Insurance and held by Adventist Risk Management, to offer Moore as part of a settlement, to keep the matter out of court. But the General Conference determined that 20 percent of the defense costs would have to be borne by Folkenberg, a fact he bitterly denounced as unfair.

It is unclear just how the news of Moore's lawsuit reached Folkenberg's fellow officers, Secretary Ralph Thompson and Treasurer Robert Rawson, in early 1999. Since the action was filed in Sacramento County, Nixon favored using the legal services of Sacramento attorney and Adventist member, Philip Hiroshima, to respond to the suit on behalf of the GC. To the surprise of many, Hiroshima found serious moral and ethical concerns about Folkenberg's behavior, as represented in the documents provided by the denomination.

After reviewing the issues with six GC vice presidents and four other officers, it was felt that a broader investigative procedure was in order. Amazingly, Folkenberg was allowed to assist in choosing those who were to compose the 19-member Ad Hoc committee — no wonder, then, that the panel came to consist of his friends on the GC Executive Committee. The group was chaired by Niels-Erik Andreasen, then president of Andrews University, and assembled for its first meeting at the Marriott Hotel at Washington's Dulles Airport. I had been tipped off that the first meeting would convene on January 25.

The idea of my General Conference president coming under judgment affected me deeply, as I painfully recalled the Kangaroo Court that had judged me little more than four years earlier. Now Folkenberg was approaching the same age I had been when I was fired, and it seemed appropriate that I should at least go to the meeting in Northern Virginia. After all, Folkenberg had been there for me!

I found it curious, indeed, that whereas I was not permitted to discuss the composition of the group who sat in judgment against me, Folkenberg had full voice in the selection of his panel. Whereas I was forbidden to have my attorney present at my sentencing, Folkenberg was flanked by two attorneys. At my hearing Mittleider had brought his long-time friend Barbara Middag to record the proceedings. At Folkenberg's tribunal, no recording was made—either audio or stenographic. Furthermore, while the *Washington Post* and the *Los Angeles Times* had been apprised of my situation by General Conference employees, no such notice was sent regarding the accusations against Folkenberg. So I personally phoned these large newspapers and told them of the meeting at the Marriott. Certainly, the General Conference had simply forgotten this minor item in the tumult of trying a president. As a layman, I was happy to do my part to assist in opening up the process to the transparent view of the Adventist public.

Naturally, the media was not permitted inside the inner sanctum conference room, but the reporters were given a spin by Folkenberg's private attorneys, who served as his bodyguards and also met with reporters from the *Adventist Review* and GC Communication Department. William Johnsson, *Adventist Review* editor and Folkenberg's long-time personal friend, with Folkenberg's input had been named a member of the Ad Hoc Committee. The situation reeked of conflict of interest between Johnsson's duties as a journalist and his role in determining the fate of the Church's sitting top executive. If ever a man should have re-cused himself from a panel, Johnsson should have done so here!

Not surprisingly, secular media coverage of Folkenberg's struggles played a key role in his fate. News outlets across the country published disclosures of the world leader's conflicts of interest, inappropriate busi-ness associations, and misuse and abuse of his office of president. Of par-ticular note was the placement in the *Washington Post* of news of Folken-berg's shenanigans between the news of US President Bill Clinton's rela-tionship with Monica Lewinsky and the illicit liaisons of an errant Baptist minister by the surname of Lyon.

After two full 12-hour days of deliberation, where the Ad Hoc com-mittee heard the detailed findings of attorney Hiroshima and presen-tations by Folkenberg and his GC-compensated private attorneys, the group recommended that the GC Executive Committee be convened to hear the matter and to take a vote of confidence on Folkenberg's ability to continue in leadership.

On the following day, January 27, 10 world division presidents joined the GC Administrative Committee (ADCOM) and accepted the Ad Hoc report. Because Folkenberg refused to resign, it was decided to call a full GC Executive Committee to review the Moore lawsuit as well as the Ad Hoc group's report.

For six weeks the *Adventist Review* provided no information about the momentous proceedings, but finally broke the silence with a guarded disclosure about the James Moore suit. On February 26, 1999, attorneys for Folkenberg and Moore reached a settlement agreement.Then, three days later, on March 1, Folkenberg's resignation became final, though he had tendered it in a letter dated February 7. He then delivered a bitter, 15-minute statement to the accelerated Spring Committee meeting, in which he complained that the Church had "abandoned" him and that certain facts in the case were not accurately reported.

Again, I drew comparisons to my own termination—one on which Folkenberg had a keen influence. I had received no financial assistance, either from Church funds or Church-held insurance, and though the Church engaged high-powered attorneys, I was not once offered legal assistance. I was terminated, and all benefits were withdrawn within a week of my final date of Church employment.

By contrast, the Church by no means left Folkenberg unemployed! An arrangement was made to link him back up with his former employer, the Carolina Conference, where he could work with his brother, who had also resigned under strange circumstances from his post as the Chief Financial Officer (CFO) for the Global Mission department of the General Conference.

The brothers were pressing on with a real estate development venture at Smith Mountain Lake in Virginia, which would raise the funds necessary for Robert Folkenberg to pay James Moore the remaining $800,000 (approximately) due from the legal settlement. Folkenberg during that time never missed a day of denominational pay, while garnering huge profits from his sideline project in Virginia.

Was it believed that Folkenberg did comparatively less damage to the name of the Church than I, by his conspicuous conflicts of interest and abuses as president of the world body of Seventh-day Adventists?

Folkenberg said that he tendered his resignation to G. Ralph Thompson, secretary of the GC Executive Committee, "to avoid pain and conflict to my family and the Church I love." The full text of his statement was read at a specially called meeting of the Church's World Headquarters in Silver Spring, Maryland, as follows:

> From my early childhood as the son of missionary parents in Inter-America, to my ministry as General Conference President, my entire life has been tirelessly and single-mindedly devoted to advancing the message and mission of the Seventh-day Adventist Church. However, over the last few weeks it has become apparent to me that the controversy surrounding the allegations of James E. Moore, made in the context of a lawsuit against the church and me, is detracting from God's work. While I have repeatedly and publicly acknowledged mistakes in dealings with Mr. Moore I rejoice that the integrity of my motives has not been called into question. However, to avoid additional pain and conflict to my family and the church I love I am removing myself from the controversy by tendering my resignation through you to the General Conference Executive Committee. I will continue to give my all to advancing the mission of the church and I pray that through this action the church can maintain its focus on the task the Lord has entrusted to us.

Sometimes I find it helps to try to articulate one's feelings by journaling them. So, with the full emotion of the moment flooding over me, I over me, I sat down that February day and wrote a response to "Robert Folkenberg, Former President, General Conference of Seventh-day Adventists."

Though I never mailed the letter, I did keep it. Allow me here to share an abbreviated version of the basic text:

Dear Bob:

It's the 8th of February as I write this letter to you. You'll always remember this day! As you can appreciate, writing a letter such as this requires much prayerful thought. This will, however, likely never be mailed to you. As I pulled up earlier today a two-page report from the Adventist News Network, I was unable to forget how this same propaganda forum had launched a methodic destruction of my own good name four years ago this past December. There I saw your photo as you made a statement concerning your resignation as president of the General Conference to the GC staff. Recognizing there are many similarities, yet great gulfs of difference between your situation and mine, nevertheless I suspect, more than most, that I can empathize with you. I know firsthand the hurt of being jerked from a position of service, where I felt my work was not done; the isolation from former friends; the evil imaginings that make an already hurtful attack even more painful. We both faced a tribunal. At mine you appointed your personal friends and those of Mittleider. At your judgment, at the Dulles Marriott Hotel, you were able to pick your allies. I was not permitted to have an

You tried to have me disfellowshipped from the church, but like you I am still considered a member in good and regular standing. Now that you have experienced the heartbreak of separation from a position you desperately sought and the political power that fed your personal corruption, is it too much for me to hope that you will feel the inspiration of God's Holy Spirit to offer to me an apology of reconciliation for the cruel treatment you inflicted, simply because you disapproved of the way I carried out my assigned function for the Church?

Sincerely,

Your Forgiving Brother in Christ

With his political connections Folkenberg is today operating a high-profile evangelistic ministry that brings in huge amounts of Adventist dollars each year and disburses them throughout the world. Yes, he has suffered from his fall, but he has fully rehabilitated himself by reinventing himself as a public evangelist — for which he has a true gift.

If only the Church were as charitable toward those who call the church *internally* to repentance.

Chapter 15:
Where Do We Go From Here?

With only short warning, at the end of 1994 we had found ourselves again searching through the ashes of our lives, trying to determine how to get back on our feet. It reminded me of the home we had lost nearly 30 years before in Chile. A glaring difference was that when our home burned then, friends surrounded us and helped us carry on. But now our friends had disappeared, and we were on our own.

Years have passed now, and the leaders' cruelty and lies stand, without apologies, without any evidence of Monday-morning conscience.

It took me several days after losing my job for reality to soak in. I recall sitting in my room early on Sabbath mornings, working out the fact that I would be forever unwelcome at General Conference activities, just five miles away. I had come within five years of retirement, and had been watching my colleagues leave with honors and little farewell fellowships. I realized that my own departure would always be associated with hostility. I can still picture Vice President Phil Follett visiting each

GC department, repeating the fatal account of the monstrous evil I had supposedly committed.

I struggled to put meaning to what had happened, in the bigger scheme of things, and thought of the falsely accused and humiliated Jesus, who was crucified by the General Conference of His day. But even as my spiritual musings began to form a reality I could embrace, I knew I had to earn a living and keep food on the table. My salary and health insurance were ending, and the Church had no unemployment insurance. At this time my father's drive and determination inspired me to move forward.

Employment offers began to come in—after all, the economy was booming. A friend at nearby Columbia Union College invited me to teach accounting and related topics in an evening MBA program. Great! But the GC was not through with me yet. Official spokespeople quickly exerted political pressure, and the invitation was revoked.

So for the first time in my life I urgently began sending out résumés—a tough sell at age 56, when my one and only employer refused to give me a letter of recommendation.

Still I sent out more than 100 résumés to companies with openings, but only two called me for interviews—small surprise, when the GC was in a position to caution them that I was a troublesome man.

At any rate, over a period of more than a month, no more job offers came through. At last my son, Sam, who with my encouragement some years before had established a small certified public accounting (CPA) practice, urged me to come work with him.

I found the practice of public accounting quite different from managing a worldwide, multi-office program with the Church's Auditing

Service. If both of us were to survive economically, I had to work fast and meet demanding schedules. Fortunately, I had no debt except for a small mortgage on our home, so I continued working with my son for nearly four years. Then, in early 1999, one of our large clients informed us that they would no longer be needing our services.

Though Sam was willing to let me stay on despite the reduced income, we would have both gone hungry. So once again I sent out résumés, this time with no references to years of schooling or anything that would betray my 60 years of age. I also left out any and all references to my employment by the Adventist Church.

This was a time when accountants were in demand, and three solid job offers came in. All offered greater earnings than my work in our little Maryland accounting office, and all offered health care and retirement benefits. But they all were far from my home, and at last I opted for a job in Northern Virginia, a 45-minute commute (when traffic was light) around the Washington beltway. My new boss agreed that I could have flex-time, so I would leave home at 4:45 a.m. and return about 2 p.m. I became the commercial accounts manager in this large CPA firm and enjoyed work and responsibilities that recognized my years of experience. It was so good to feel appreciated and accepted.

We had proven that God was looking out for us, though at times the meal barrel seemed empty. We never missed a meal, nor did we have to wear threadbare clothing. People we had never met before would shower us with little gifts of money, just in time to meet financial deadlines. We felt like Elijah, fed by ravens in the Old Testament. God sent us just enough to let us know He loved and cared for us.

For almost two years I felt confident in my work and enjoyed Sabbaths off. I developed tremendous relationships with company clients and fellow staff members. I noticed that the company had begun building its business in government contracting—a natural growth area for a company near the capital. But I did not feel comfortable with this kind of work—frankly, it was boring beyond belief. But soon I was caught up in this new work, supervising young accountants. Many long-term clients, however, felt disenfranchised because they were not getting the attention they had once received from us.

By February 2002 I decided to go back to work with Sam, to help him with new business accounts that had come his way. But as I returned to my desk with Sam, I found that clients I had been serving with my former employer now wanted to transfer their business to Sam's company. We now continue to bask in this windfall of blessing. Our practice is now more successful than at any time in its history.

It is a secular work, but the kinship and acceptance with our international clientele from Egypt, Latin America, France, Greece, Iran, and Africa is something I never felt in Church work. I've just turned 70 years old and retirement will come in good time, but I still look forward to going to work each and every morning.

Charlotte's life and mine revolve around our little Maryland church, between the shadows of the General Conference and the Review & Herald Publishing Association, where I serve as an elder and Charlotte is head deaconess and music coordinator. We give our tithes and offerings, though not into coffers that could finance litigation or character assassination.

(Chapter continues on Page 133)

FROM CHARLOTTE'S PERSPECTIVE:

The offices of the General Conference (GC) were quiet back in 1994, as the Annual Council meetings opened. I was seated at my desk in Treasury, assisting missionaries as they prepared for service in the Far Eastern Division.

Suddenly David appeared, looking as if he'd just seen a ghost. He asked me to read a document he'd been given by General Conference attorneys. As I read the accusations made against him by a now middle-aged woman who years before as a troubled teen had called me her "best friend," I felt like a bolt of lightning had hit me! David and I prayed together in the chapel, then walked to meet with Vice President Kenneth Mittleider, in his office. I felt comforted that he and GC-employed attorney, Walter Carson, had been assigned to investigate these lurid allegations, and would show us compassion and kindness.

But they greeted us coldly, with countenances set and hard, demanding that David resign immediately, and when he refused, things only got worse.

Back in my office, David and I could look through the windows into the committee room, as another General Conference vice president, Phil Follett, gathered various groups of employees and told them of the accusations against David, of his refusal to resign, and of his imminent in-house trial.

David had been told to clear out of his office, cancel all travel, and surrender his keys, and security staff was told to supervise him at all times whenever he was in the General Conference offices.

Friends began to stop by my office to console me. Anguish filled my heart, as I reflected on what this would mean to our children, who knew of our sacrifices on behalf of the church. From the beginning we had dedicated our married lives without reservation to the Adventist Church, and it seemed unbearable to leave our mission in this way. David and I had always worked as a team. We had never aspired to the upper echelon cliques of the Church and lacked the social recognition of those in top leadership. David had no close golf buddies among the officers. He simply loved his home and quiet times with the family, and worked tirelessly to advance the causes in which he believed.

As the days passed, I watched as the one I loved—the one who had always had so much energy, drive, and vision in his responsibilities for the Lord—sat in our living room, staring blankly at the wall. He had no idea, now, how he would make a living, but he would still put his arms around me and say, "Charlotte, you don't have to stay on and work at the General Conference. I know God will provide for us." Grateful for his understanding, I turned in my resignation.

Then came the "Kangaroo Court," with its Gestapo-like proceedings and an ultimatum—that I could either defend David verbally, or sit beside him as a silent witness. The GC brethren would not permit me to do both.

Mittleider, meanwhile, recognized that contrary to plan, David was not going to resign under fire, and Mittleider's anger visibly seethed. I knew as well as David that the affair Beth Adels was describing could never have taken place. Though she said she had met illicitly with my husband in Portland, Tennessee, 12 years before, I distinctly remembered traveling, myself, with David during that time—something the GC officers did not know and Beth in her confused state of mind had forgotten to tell them. In fact, David and I had visited with Beth and her parents in the course of our travels together. I told Mittleider that we had traveled together in the family car, and that we were enjoying the time we had to spend together. David simply would not have had the time or op-portunity to do anything like what Beth was describing through psychiatrically induced false memory syndrome.

But as I shared this information at the in-house hearing, Mittleider roughly interrupted me and shouted, "You're lying!" In turn, I told him that I recognized a rigged hearing when I saw one, but even so, I was pledged to tell the absolute truth, as I knew it.

Beth Adels sat in the meeting room that day as I spoke. I looked directly at her, but she would clutch her Kleenex box and refuse to meet my gaze. As part of the charade, both David and I had been forbidden to speak to her or to communicate in any way.

Here sat the same woman who had come to live in our Singapore home, troubled, confused, and even suicidal. Her parents feared for her life, and David and I had agreed to let her come to our house—because we wanted to be of help. I recalled spending hours, listening to her confused reasoning, devoting time I could have been spending with our own children.

Many times, in fact, she had told me that I was her "best friend." She considered me a confidant, but even then her imagination would run riot. It was by no means inconceivable to me that in the intervening years, she and her therapist might have "recovered" false memories about that time, or about our visit in 1982. But I knew then, as certainly as I know now, that David has been incorruptible in his financial and marital commitments. Not once in 35 years had anyone mentioned anything remotely suggestive about David's behavior. But strange things can happen in confused minds—I suppose there's always a first time.

Now I fully expected that this hand-picked "jury" would vote that a troubled woman's story was more believable than my husband's, and so it happened that on Christmas Eve, 1994, he was terminated "effective immediately," but in the charitable spirit of the holidays, his salary and our health-care benefits were extended for one more week. We immediately invoked our rights, by policy, to be heard by an unbiased "grievance committee," but our petition was denied.

Our last recourse, it seemed, was to take our case to a secular tribunal. We wanted justice. We wanted to find out what was really going on. But this was not to be. For seven long years, the highly compensated lawyers hired by the General Conference fought—not to present facts, but to keep the case from going to trial! Our son, Sam, and I would sit in the judge's chambers, hearing lie, upon lie, upon lie, as the lawyers tried to discredit the auditor who, over the years, had called so many of the Church's actions into question. The one-sided depositions (our GC persecutors were never deposed) intentionally hurt our children with their unmerciful grilling.

Humiliating as it was, we did not allow this crushing treatment to deny us eternity—we held onto our faith in the goodness of God and His blessings.

Of five children in my family, I am the only who has remained faithful to the Church, though in recent years an older brother has given his heart to Christ. My oldest brother has asked me, "Why do you remain in such a church?" I have told him that the Church is made up of frail—even dishonest and corrupt—human beings. We are not perfect, I told him, but we can always trust God and His perfect Word. I still believe that.

I love the Adventist message and am committed to following it all the days of my life. The Mittleiders and Folkenbergs of this world cannot steal my crown! I truly believe that whatever tragedies we suffer here on earth will pale to insignificance when compared with dwelling forever with Jesus.

Many miracles have been wrought on our behalf, for which we thank our Best Friend, Jesus. I have also learned that there are "true friends" in the here and now, and for each I am truly thankful.

Our Church still has much to learn on the matter of loving, rather than condemning. I thank God, He is my Judge!

Our loving little church home invites me from time to time to speak from the pulpit. Clearly, there are two distinct parts of the Adventist Church—the manipulative elite and the cheerful, charitable majority. Not all Church practices are godly or divinely initiated. We recognize that skilled spin doctors are alive and well at the highest levels of Church administration—and that's just the way things are in an imperfect world.

I once believed that it was impossible to be an effective Church member, without engaging in Church politics. Now I purposely stay out of politics, in both the spiritual and secular realms.

But it's hard to ignore the less-than-resolute reformation the aging Jan Paulsen's administration has brought our Church. I know that the ethical behavior of many Adventist leaders pains him, and from time to time he has spoken out for change. But the fact remains that without his nod, Folkenberg could not have stayed on the Church payroll.

Clearly Ted Wilson is now maneuvering to be in the right place for a return of the Wilson dynasty to the top rung of GC administration, and I believe that unless cultural opposition arises from outside North America, he will be elected on the first ballot, though he has never once served as a local Church pastor. He has carefully made the rounds of overseas service and institutions in the U.S. to give his résumé just the right look. Meanwhile, Paulsen goes through the motions as a figurehead. Recently he appeared on a media presentation, discussing the spiritual healing needed after the ethnic holocaust in Rwanda. He said we must all be prepared to forgive, because we all need forgiveness. His interpretation of who this includes, of course, is selective—and the same old animus of political expediency continues to drive the machinery of Adventism, if not its ideology.

We have learned over these years that many others have suffered termination, alienation, and destruction, without cause, at the hands of Adventist ministers and Church leaders—their only crime being that they did not follow the prevailing political winds.

It had been Charlotte's and my hope and prayer that the litigation we brought would help bring change in the Church. But the judicial system in America is also broken. I remember the rather personal words of Judge Turner, who first examined my case. He asked the Church attorneys point blank, "If the General Conference had castrated Mr. Dennis for his offenses, would you still try to hide behind First Amendment privilege to avoid paying him damages?"

They answered, "No." But I know that even if the Church had arranged to have me murdered, it still would have argued that it had a First Amendment privilege to do so, in the pursuit of its autonomous practice of religion.

I continue to ask, "How is it possible to commit crimes in the name of religious freedom, without being held accountable? How can an errant Church continue to enjoy tax-exempt status?" These questions apply to all churches.

As things stand today, virtually all Adventist Church employee receives some sort of credential, and by showing these to a court they can turn almost any complaint against them into an "ecclesiastical matter." Yet the Church has the liberty to bring legal actions at any time against anyone it chooses, including its own members.

Perhaps the greatest disappointment to us, from the judge's ruling to immunize the Church from our civil suit, was that the internal corruption that led to my termination would be effectively hidden from public scrutiny. Had the details become known sooner, Folkenberg would probably not have been reelected in 1995, and significant changes could have been brought in the Church's political system.

There is, however, one heartening memory of the trauma we endured. I hasten to note that our suffering was inflicted by frail humans. It was not "the Church" or Church policy that hounded us from office. Zealous, misguided individuals simply felt I needed to be removed, and with bitter efficiency did it in the most ruthless of ways—ignoring the spirit of an otherwise gracious Church policy.

A precious few did reach out their hands of fellowship to us after we left Church employment—mostly unheralded people who contributed to our costs of litigation and helped us meet our other personal needs. Others, in the manner of Christ, simply reached out just to be helpful, supportive, and kind.

At the top of this deeply appreciated list are the names of Francis and Sue Wernick. Francis would call me, just to share a bit of brightness and love on a Friday evening. Or they would drop by the office with veggies from their garden. Bill Shea, who contributed the Foreword to this manuscript, is a world-renowned Old Testament scholar who had recently retired from the GC Biblical Research offices. He encouraged us and offered his friendship.

Another friend during that difficult time was Erwin Gane, a prolific writer and former college theology professor, who had retired from the GC and now lives in California.

Our loving little family has stood together through it all. After nearly 50 years of marriage, Charlotte and I still enjoy one another's company. How grateful we are to have our children geographically and emotionally close to us. Sam and I still work together. He has suffered many health problems, some serious, but lately he has been basking in heaven's healing and is close to Jesus. Cheryl and her family live near our offices and often share little Emma with us, our youngest grandchild. She is precocious and extremely alert for her tender years.

Other things have improved, for time is a great healer. No longer do our fellow Church workers dash away (most of them now seem too old to run, anyway) when they see us coming. Some still shun us, but their attacks are losing steam. A former missionary friend recently phoned and told me that he put no stock whatever in the charges of sexual misconduct — that from our years of association, he had never seen anything in my behavior that would lead him to believe such a charge.

Slowly the message is coming through that had there been any provable evidence at all against me, the General Conference would have saved itself millions of dollars and simply allowed the case to go to trial.

Yes, we have lost most of those we once considered our friends, but are thankful for new ones — a new and loving local church family, and many non-Adventist contacts we otherwise would not have met.

So we press on. Scars remain from the hurtfulness of those who still feel that they benefit the cause of Adventism by vilifying us. The Church will ultimately believe what it chooses, but the fact remains that no one involved in my destruction has yet sought my forgiveness, though as far as possible I have forgiven them.

God declares that He will care for any "vengeance," and, time after time, as in the case of Folkenberg's fall, we have seen His intervening hand. We are more than convinced that we must move forward, ministering to others, and holding on for dear life to Jesus Christ.